BACK

TO THE SEA

THE TRUE STORY

OF

SOUTHPORT

by

Frank Bamford

Photography by Colin Bamford

First published in 2001
by Frank Bamford

© copyright Frank Bamford 2001
ISBN 0 9517225 4 9

Typeset by Northern Writers Advisory Services, Sale, Cheshire
M33 4DN

Printed by Intype (London) Ltd, Wimbledon, London SW19 4HE

CONTENTS

ILLUSTRATIONS

Front cover

Maps

Photographs

To Joyce who enticed me to Southport.

INTRODUCTION

Since I first came to Southport four or five years ago, I have become enthralled by its many attractions, fascinated by its unique-
ness and intrigued by its history. I have read various local books
and particularly enjoyed a number of picture book histories published in recent years. However, I have been left with a strong
sense of discontent about the apparently accepted simple story of
a wealthy resort which scorned the opportunity of becoming a really popular seaside holiday place similar, say, to Blackpool.

This account, so simplified as to represent the town almost as a
resort without history, has always seemed to me to ignore the very
obvious and indeed hugely obtruding physical characteristic
which so clearly distinguishes Southport from all the major popular resorts, i.e. the existence of a wide strip of land stretching between a quarter and half a mile between the promenade and the
sea. Much of this broad space has of course been developed with
attractive gardens and parks, a major fun fair and a vast marine
lake. Yet it is far from a normal situation for a resort, with its glit-
tering Lord Street shops, to be such a long, long walk from anything like a beach.

So the intriguing historical questions, which soon loomed large,
were – How did this unique phenomenon arise? What was the impact of the underlying twist of nature upon the growth of the town
and on the related attitude of its citizens to living there and to attracting and receiving visitors? What indeed was the overall effect
on the town of its evident desertion by the ocean?

All these intriguing questions presented me with a very clear
signal that there was ample material hidden somewhere for a very
special local history which unravelled the evident mysteries and
sought to tell the true story in proper sequence, decade by decade
perhaps.

It was soon clear that the only reliable and sustained sources
were the contemporary accounts in the pages of the local press.
So this book is essentially the result of patient researches in the
columns of *The Visiter* – first published in 1844 – held on micro-
fiche in the Local History section in Southport Library. They have
revealed a fascinating story which I have retold in this book.
(Without the willing assistance of the staff of the library, this book
could not have been published.)

Yet properly to understand all that has happened in this western corner of England in the past two centuries, it is essential also to see it all in the perspective of the national picture of immense economic, industrial and social change. So, as I have done in my other local histories, I have sought to explain how these vast upheavals have, in each period, impacted on the life and development of the town. This is not to suggest that Southport has been a mere weathervane turning in response to national winds, but only that its own very special story has been to some extent affected by wider forces.

This is emphatically not a picture book as such, but it includes quite a number of pictures. These have been included only to illuminate the major development in each period where they are interspersed in the text. For instance, it is hardly possible to appreciate the immense explosion of wealth in Southport in the railway age of the third quarter of the nineteenth century without witnessing together some of the numerous examples of the splendours of mid-Victorian architecture.

March 2001

1
BEGINNINGS: THE CANAL AGE

Two hundred years ago Southport barely existed. From the principal village in the area, North Meols, now Churchtown, a little road ran south eastwards to Roe Lane, curving eventually south west to the sea along what is today Manchester Road. All around the coast for hundreds of yards inland was the domain of sandhills with a few small houses, mainly fishermens' cottages, almost hidden in them near the shore.

The subsequent story of Southport has been governed by two factors of overriding importance – the sea and the immense development of southern Lancashire in the Industrial Revolution and beyond. For the town has, of course, always been by the sea but has never grown much by its own industry and commerce. Not possessing the favourable conditions which made possible the vast growth of the cotton textile industry, i.e. the running water and coal in particular, it has always been quite remote from the main centres of population and difficult of access from them until the growth of industry spurred the development of new transport systems.

In the eighteenth century very few people travelled more than a few miles from their own homes. Unless you were affluent enough to own a horse or even a horse and cart or carriage, a walk of four or five miles to the nearest market town was probably your limit, although towards the end of the century a small number of excursions in horse drawn carriages were organised.

This basic fact of dependence on the horse severely limited the scope for the growth of industrial and commercial enterprises, both in relation to the acquisition of raw materials, including coal, and also in respect of the scope for selling products and widening the market. Small wonder, then, that the development of the textile industries was in the hands of itinerant merchants who carried the yarn and cloth from one production stage to another and then to market.

Yet it was long ago appreciated that a horse could pull goods much more effectively and efficiently in a boat along water. So already in the eighteenth century this simple concept was applied to utilising the great natural resource of our rivers by making them more navigable with the construction of locks, bridges and even aqueducts. (What an amazing and intriguing device is a lock

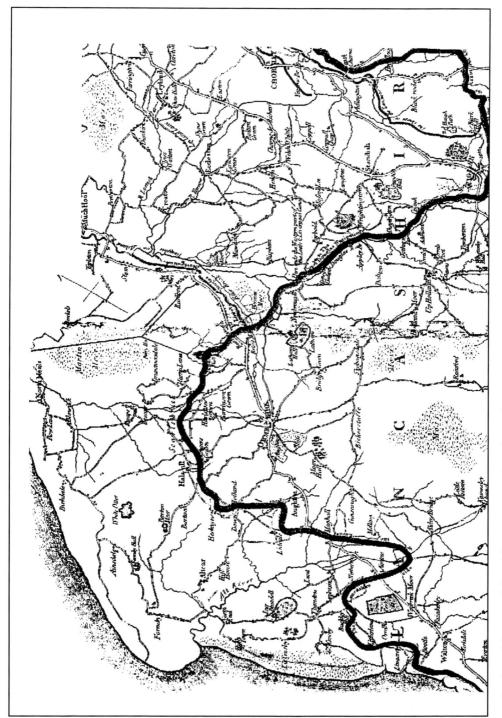

Leeds and Liverpool Canal (western section) and Douglas Navigation, 1795. Note that North Meols, Birkdale, Scarisbrick, Tarleton and Much Hoole are named but not Southport.

Baines 1824 Map of the coast from North Meols to Hesketh Bank. Note Crossens by the sea.

which can be used, by applying modest human effort, to harness the force of gravity to move a boat up a hill or manage its descent down a fast flowing stream!) In Yorkshire the Aire and Calder Navigation was a major early example of this magical method of transport.

Quite early in the eighteenth century a similar, although more modest project was developed on Southport's doorstep, inspired in part by the need to improve the movement of materials such as coal and limestone. The scheme involved making the River Douglas navigable from Wigan to the coast near Hesketh Bank a few miles north of Southport. After more than twenty years of debate and development, the waterway was finally opened in 1742. Interestingly in the light of developments in the next two centuries, one of its objectives was to facilitate the movement of materials and goods across the mouth of the Ribble to the Fylde area noted for being quite inaccessible – even more so than the Southport area! A principal feature of the project was the building of thirteen locks.

The story of the project is well recounted in Mike Clarke's book on the Leeds and Liverpool Canal, which tells also of a proposal discussed in the 1730's for an alternative route from Rufford to the sea across Martin Mere to Crossens, which would have been six miles shorter, although more expensive to construct. One great advantage of the Crossens route was that "the greater tidal range at Crossens would give more reliable access to sea-going vessels".

Inhabitants of Southport, even those who have lived all their lives in the area, may well rub their eyes at the words "greater tidal range at Crossens" now well over a mile from the sea. Yet local maps, at least well up to the end of the eighteenth century, do show Crossens close to the shore and legend has it the sea actually approached Churchtown near the Botanic Gardens area.

We may note in passing that the fact that Britain is an island or group of islands with nowhere more than a hundred miles from the sea significantly multiplied the benefit of making our rivers navigable. For if a horse-drawn vehicle could carry goods to the sea, a wind-borne boat could carry them much further – around the coast or even abroad.

Thus it was that the next and quite revolutionary transport age developed - the building of the canals. The first major new waterway was initially in fact an inland affair built by 1760 by the Duke of Bridgewater to carry coal from his mines at Worsley into Manchester which had already grown into an industrial city and needed fuel for heating homes and factories. The pioneering canal was later extended south-west to join the Mersey estuary at Runcorn by a long and meandering route following the contour lines and so avoiding the building of locks.

Eventually the Bridgewater Canal became of major importance to Southport by opening up a canal route to Manchester. This followed the construction of the great Leeds and Liverpool Canal which, crossing from Yorkshire at Skipton, connected major Lancashire towns like Blackburn to Wigan whence it followed a westerly route, again on the contour lines, to within five miles of Southport near Scarisbrick before proceeding on a gentle southerly line to Liverpool. The River Douglas Navigation, partially "canalised" (i.e. improved by the construction of lengths of canal alongside it) eventually became a branch of the Leeds - Liverpool.

Of course, the major improvements in the transport of goods in the eighteenth century did not happen without great economic stimulus. Particularly during the latter part of the century the pace of mechanical invention in the textile industries quickened remarkably. First spinning and later weaving, with cotton ahead of wool, passed from hand operation, mainly in people's houses in the villages and small towns, to workshops and factories which were constructed by the moneyed classes – mainly the very merchants who had previously organised the progress of material through the different stages of manufacture in various places.

Power for the new machines came from running water driving water wheels, a fact which accounts for the location of the factories along the flanks of the Pennines, spurring the growth of numerous cotton towns in Lancashire and Yorkshire. Towards the end of the century the development of the steam engine enabled textile manufacture to grow away from the streams and rivers and particularly to a place like Preston and, overwhelmingly, Manchester. The latter, which had already become a great commercial centre for the cotton trade by 1800, was establishing itself as the first great industrial city in the world, dominating the world market for cotton yarn with its huge spinning mills which can still be seen at Ancoats. So the city grew from 70,000 people in 1800 to 300,000 by 1850. Other Lancashire towns like Blackburn, Burnley, Wigan and Bolton, also grew apace. Oldham went from 22,000 in 1801 to 72,000 in 1851.

The great port for the world cotton trade was Liverpool, which, of course, was the essential reason for the construction of the Leeds and Liverpool Canal connecting the developing industrial areas of Lancashire and Yorkshire to the sea. Liverpool was naturally the entry point for the raw cotton necessarily imported from the southern states of America, but this trade was quite modest until the manufacturing explosion in Manchester and other towns in the nineteenth century. (The consumption of cotton yarn grew from 150,000lbs in 1820 to 650,000lbs in 1850 and 1,100,000lbs in 1870.)

However, Liverpool was already a large and well-to-do port by 1800 on the back of the huge development of the slave trade, for which it became the main European port, overtaking Bristol and London during the eighteenth century. The trade involved ships from Liverpool taking goods such as textiles from the north and metal goods, including guns, from the Midlands to west Africa, trading them effectively for slaves which were carried in abominable conditions to the Caribbean and southern U.S.A. whence the ships brought a variety of products such as tobacco, sugar and raw cotton back to Liverpool. Before this awful trade was officially abolished by Parliament in 1807 (though some trading went on well after that), many Liverpool "merchants" had become very wealthy. In the later decades of the eighteenth century, typically two ships a week would sail from Liverpool for Africa whence they carried an average of some 250 slaves each to the Americas – about 25,000 a year. Each slave was worth about £50 or more like £5,000 in today's values. So one can understand why there was great opposition the abolition of the business. It is not so easy to understand that so many supposedly civilised people had been caught up in the terrible trade.

What, however, is beyond doubt is that Liverpool had, by virtue of the slave trade, become a great port and a substantial town by 1800. Its present magnificent town hall was built as early as 1760, the third town hall in fact. In the nineteenth century it would become the focal port for the huge textile business of Lancashire and west Yorkshire.

This, then, is the new fast commercial world into which Southport was born at the beginning of the new century.

The story of the early development of the Southport area in the late eighteenth and early nineteenth centuries has been well told – for instance in Harry Foster's *Southport – A Pictorial History.*

The ancient parish of North Meols was centred in what is now the village of Churchtown with its church, hall and two coaching inns, just a few miles from today's Southport centre. As the attractions of sea-bathing became more evident and accessible to a small but growing fraction of the Lancashire population it became apparent that the beach at Southport was more attractive if only because it was less exposed to Ribble mud, and the first little hotel was built in 1798 near what is now the south end of Lord Street.

By 1800 the population of the whole North Meols area was no more then 2,500 with only a few hundreds in what is now the town of Southport in a few score houses built along the sandhills in the area which became Lord Street. For the next twenty years growth was quite slow so that in 1821 North Meols included only just over 3,000 inhabitants of which Southport probably accounted for about 500.

It was in the following twenty years that a great spurt developed with North Meols rising to over 8,000 and Southport accounting for 2161 residents and 1185 visitors, according to a contemporary report. By 1851 the numbers had grown steadily to 9,300 for all North Meols including a grand total of 4,200 for Southport.

How then do we account for this accelerated growth from 1820 to 1850? Well, it is of course partly a reflection of the growth of the industrial population of Lancashire with the associated rise in wealth of the owning and managerial classes. But, above all, it was a question of access. In this period the only semblance of the

St Cuthbert's Church.

Bold Arms Hotel.

Cottages and Church.

Churchtown Village has changed little since the eighteenth century. All these buildings are older than anything in Southport.

commercial provision of passenger transport was the skeletonic stage coach system. There was still no decent road even into Southport, although a few stage coaches made their way there. However, the industry – driven creation of the canal network for moving materials and goods created a spin-off benefit for those quite few individuals who could afford the time and money to travel to the coast.

Even so, the benefit was quite limited during the decades from the 1770's during which the Leeds-Liverpool Canal was progressively opened – reaching Blackburn, for instance in 1810. It was only when the link to Manchester was completed in 1820 by the opening of the branch from Wigan to Leigh that the passenger traffic to Southport really began to take off.

From inland Lancashire towns like Wigan, Blackburn, Burnley and Manchester itself, people were able to disembark at Scarisbrick and transfer to horse-drawn carriages and carts for the five-mile trip to the seaside. Visitors also came from the Liverpool area which had its own seaside attractions. It was a very slow means of transport but it did widen the range of possibilities.

Thus Southport itself had changed but little by the 1820's with buildings confined to what is now the southern half of Lord Street with substantial houses along the eastern side and a row behind it. By 1850, however, when the railway age (of which much more in the next chapter) had barely begun, both sides of Lord Street had been quite fully developed. A private promenade had been built for a quarter of a mile from the south to reach the Victoria Baths with new links to Lord Street, i.e. Neville Street and Sea Bank Road. East Bank Street, Chapel Street and Hoghton Street were developing, as well as the area south of East Bank Street.

It is important to stress at this point that the only people who could visit Southport before the railway age, let alone build houses and settle there, were those who were relatively affluent enough to be able to spare the significant amount of time and money to overcome the problem of the distance from the large industrial areas and towns. This distance was too great for the mill owners to commute on a regular basis, yet not too far for a small number of them to establish holiday and retirement homes. Already, however, the tone was set for the characteristically large scale of the impressive dwellings, which have dominated the heart of the town until today.

An astonishing token of the wealth of the local inhabitants ishat

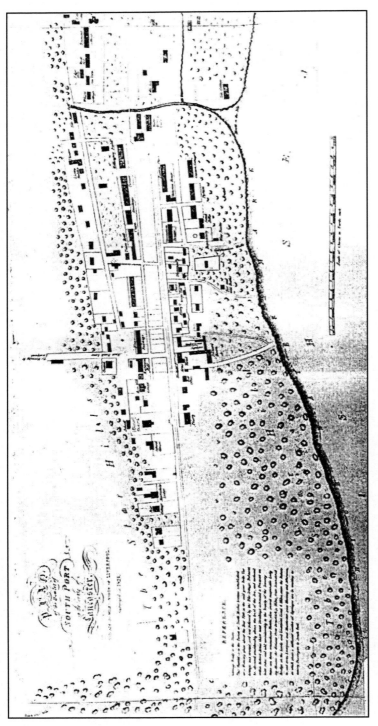

Map of Southport 1824. Text under heading REFERENCE reads: "CARRIAGE ROADS TO THE SHORE. This Hamlet is in the parish of North Meols. Became a watering place about the year 1798; in the said year Belle Vue Cottage was erected and was followed by the Nile Cottage and Belmont Cottage elevated considerably above the level of the sea and enclosed within distinct areas. These neat dwellings command a prospect on both sides and add considerably to the beauty of the scenery. There are three commodious Hotels, also several respectable Lodging Houses. The distance from Ormskirk is 9 miles; from Scarisbrick Bridge on the Leeds and Liverpool 6 miles." Note the surrounding and invasive presence of sandhills on which the two sides of Lord Street were built with a marshy hollow between.

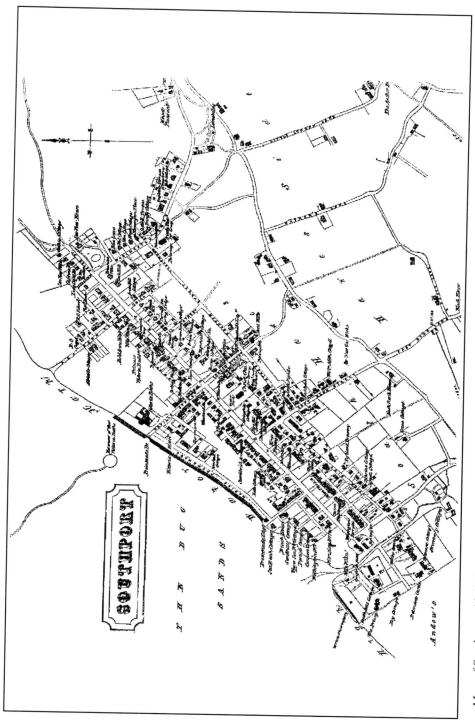

Map of Southport, 1849. Note Victoria Baths and Victoria Hotel on the Promenade, Scarisbrick Arms and Bold Arms Hotels on Lord Street, and development of "Cottages" and houses along Manchester Road towards Churchtown in the North-east.

in the early 1850's when the population of Southport, including visitors, was barely 5,000 and that of the whole North Meols parish some 10,000, they were planning to build an elegant classical town hall which was in fact opened in 1854. Such civic pride was typical of the Lancashire cotton towns in the Victorian period but rarely at such an early stage in local development.

Of course the new town hall presided in the middle of Lord Street, which, following the lines of the sandhills on which it was originally built along the sides of the marshy trough between, had already attained something of its spacious elegant appearance, consistent with the wealth of the town's early inhabitants, for which it has become famous.

Southport Town Hall.

2
RAILWAY MANIA

If the growth of Southport in the canal age of the second quarter of the century was substantial but measured, its outburst in the third quarter was hardly less than frenetic. This swift change of gear was essentially the result of the new era of transport since it was still true that the town boasted no internal engine of growth.

The canals had been constructed in a careful, almost tentative, manner after protracted discussion and deliberation, hardly surprising for the first stage of artificial means of transport development. A major enterprise like the Leeds and Liverpool was several decades in planning and construction as, quite apart from the physical problems, all kinds of novel procedures had to be organised for obtaining rights to cross private land, all involving acts of Parliament, not to mention the commercial hazards of this quite new kind of enterprise.

So when the steam engine, which had been developed in the later eighteenth century, became applied to transportation, much relevant experience in relation to forging links between towns and cities had already been gained. Much more than that, the whole economy of England had moved on with the application of steam to textile production.

Scarisbrick Arms Hotel and Lord Street (1854). Note that BROADBENT'S premises at left centre are among the very few buildings to have survived from this period.

The phenomenal expansion of the English cotton textile industry to world-wide dominance brought immense profit to a multitude of industrialists who not only required great improvements in transport to facilitate this expansion but also progressively accumulated quite unprecedented profits to invest in them.

In thirty years from the opening of the Liverpool - Manchester railway in 1830, a Railway Mania in fact developed which created the main structure of lines across England. This was the great age of venture capitalism and the exploitation of the joint stock company which soon attained a swift momentum of its own well beyond considerations of what was economically justified or commercially profitable. There was nothing like rational planning of the resulting national railway network as each group of entrepreneurs perceived a profit opportunity with little regard to what other groups were planning. So many competing lines were built that many of them proved unprofitable - the late twentieth century explosion of communications technology has been wonderfully similar.

The canals, as we have noted, were essentially organised for transport of materials and goods, but with railways, as personal wealth for investment and for travel rapidly increased, the emphasis progressively shifted to passenger transport. There was indeed competition with the canals for industrial traffic in which, perhaps surprisingly, the canals continued to prosper for many decades as their half a century of dominance had encouraged the buildings of factories along their banks in places which the railways found it difficult to reach. Yet it was the enormous potential for people to travel, for the first time in history, which the railways soon learnt to exploit and promote.

The wholly unprecedented nature of this new age of transport was nowhere more apparent than in the experience of the Great Exhibition of 1851 in London, which drew many more people of almost all classes than had been expected. In barely eight months a total of six million travellers journeyed to Hyde Park, far more than had been expected and similar to the number who have visited the Dome in the year 2000 from twice the population.

In this new era, progress came rather late to Southport but when it came its results were dramatic. The delay was not altogether surprising since the area was always somewhat detached from the industrial areas and its population was less than 10,000 by the middle of the century. The town had not set itself up as a popular resort – such a place was barely understood at the time – but rather had developed as a modest well-to-do site to which comfortable business people could repair or retire in fresh air and sea breezes.

So the first railway line did not open until 1848 connecting the town first to Waterloo and then in 1850 to Liverpool and it was not until 1855 that there was a connection to Manchester through Wigan with a direct line opening in 1862.

The impact of the railways was astonishing. From 1851 to 1881 the population of the whole North Meols area grew from 9,300 to 42,400 with Southport itself, including by then Churchtown and Crossens, registering over 32,000. By the end of the century another 16,000 people lived in Southport some of them no doubt temporarily. In the town itself the population more than trebled between 1850 and 1868 and a glance at the maps for those years clearly reveals the immense expansion in all directions with some streets of smaller houses appearing on the edge of the central area.

Within fifteen to twenty years of the opening of the route to Manchester, two other railways were being built, a line to Preston to which there was already a connection via the Wigan line, and a new line from the south end of Lord Street to Aintree and on to join the Manchester- Liverpool line near Warrington - of which much more later. So the Southport area was somewhat tardily engulfed by railway mania with sixteen stations operating at one time, more in fact than the passenger traffic could eventually bear for reasons which we shall also address.

In the meantime we should consider the nature of this great population invasion. Driving around the area at the beginning of the twenty-first century, one cannot fail to appreciate the great preponderance of substantial middle and upper class houses, many of them designed to accommodate several servants or at least a single maid to accord with the appropriate local status. Eventually of course many more modest streets of dwellings were built to house the working class people needed to serve the needs of the well to do, but the landowners who controlled the town, essentially the Scarisbricks and the Heskeths, ensured that these were sited away from the main prestigious town centre areas. Certainly there was very small scope for such working class people except that ensured by the supply and service requirements of the "superior" classes.

The greatest concentrations of great houses and mansions were developed in what were effectively wealthy suburbs to the north and south. The first was created in the 1850s and 1860s in what became known as Birkdale Park mainly between the present Birkdale station and the cliff then overlooking the beach where Rotten Row now runs. After winning a disputed inheritance, Thomas Weld-Blundell took possession of the huge site in 1848 and originally mapped out an estate in the form of concentric circles but eventually it was built in widely spaced and fairly straight streets. The original Birkdale station, on the Liverpool line, was situated further south but was moved north to serve the new great estate. Of course the sea and the beach were very close.

Perhaps inspired by this wealthy development, another major local landowner, Revd. Charles Hesketh, planned his suburban estate to the north of the town where the corporation had ideas about creating a public park among the sandhills. In 1859 Hesketh himself donated the land for the park on condition that the town council developed and maintained it as well as connecting the area to Southport's roads, water supply and services. So the landowner's apparent philanthropy was by no means entirely altruistic since the whole scheme resulted in a huge increase in land values as a wide ring of mansions was built in the late 1860s and in the 1870s, expanding to the landward or eastern side around Park Avenue, Park Crescent and Park Road.

Albert Road, the extension of Lord Street, was already by the late 1860s stretching north towards the new park and by the early 1870s great houses were built along the road to the west of the park with their gardens stretching down to the shallow cliff overlooking the beach and formidable sandhills. By 1881 the census returns showed many great houses in the area occupied by wide miscellany of upper middle class people including retired manufacturers of cotton goods and glass as well as 'merchants', solicitors, either practising or retired, justices of the peace, magistrates and so on. All these people employed several living-in servants. There were even one or two small boarding schools - Glenham House on Park Avenue had twenty-five occupants. Close by on Albert Road, the Imperial Hotel was already established.

An interesting aspect of the northern end of the promenade is indeed the curved stretch north eastward from the end of Leyland Road which arose from the fact that until well into the 1880s there was a bay of the sea extending into the coast in this area

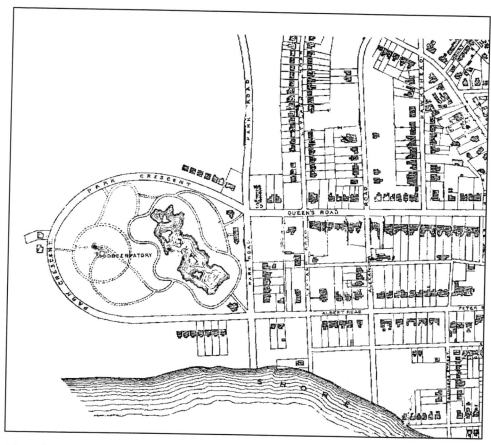

Map of Hesketh Park area in 1875. Shows early mansions on Albert Road.

right up to the grounds of the mansions on Albert Road opposite Hesketh Park. It was only a quite late recession of the sea which led to the reclamation of about half a mile of land on which was eventually built the comfortable houses along Fleetwood Road as well as the Municipal Golf Course.

All this astonishing upsurge of impressive dwellings is graphic evidence of the enormous wealth engendered in industrial Lancashire in the mid-Victorian period, enough to build the country's railway network and to enrich thousands of people who came to Southport not only to visit holiday homes or retire, but to commute to Manchester itself which was only forty-five minutes away by train and to towns like Blackburn still closer. Of course for the commercial men of Liverpool, with its huge ocean borne trade in

Early mansions on Albert Road. These mansions were the first to be built close to Hesketh Park. Their back gardens stretched down to the shallow cliff overlooking the beach where Fleetwood Road now runs. Their size became the general standard for the area, but others were bigger.

which slavery had loomed large, Southport was even more conveniently close. Compared of course to the grimy industrial and commercial towns and cities, it began to shine like a new-fashioned jewel of a place with ample space, impressive buildings, attractive shops – and the sea. There was just nowhere else like it.

Small wonder, then, that the Town Hall of 1854 was soon followed by other notable buildings culminating in 1874 in the adjacent grandiose Cambridge Hall, a municipal building for meetings and entertainments. Meanwhile in the 1860's Lord Street had been landscaped with attractive gardens.

In the same decade another major development of great significance to the town in its seaside setting was the construction of a pier. It had already become the fashion for the major resorts such as Brighton to adorn themselves with a pier, or even two, demonstrating that the main purpose was to provide an additional seaside promenade with perhaps an extra thrill and even more ozone. New leisure and entertainment facilities were provided, including fishing and boating. Initially it seems, however, that the sea-going transport connections were not of major significance, although for Southport such an objective would have been the only way of justifying such a name for a resort grown on the flattest of flat coasts.

Anyway, work on the Southport pier, an enterprise with a capital of £10,000, began in 1859 and the opening of a significant structure 1200 yards long took place in 1860. Within a few years, the need for considerable improvement was widely expressed and by 1866 a lower level extension of 240 yards had been built, a tramway installed and various other items added.

The main purpose of the 1866 extension was to make it easier for a variety of sea going vessels to use it at any state of the tide. The new length of 720 feet was arranged in six stages of 120 feet each on a different level. In 1863 a tramway was opened, resulting in a protest that it spoilt the pier as a promenade, so in 1864 it was widened and the tramway moved to the south side. There remained also a narrow promenade platform 120 feet long at the end of the main pier and parallel to the shore, which was said to be 16 feet above the sands at low tide and 25 feet at high tide.

All this, however, was not regarded as adequate by some local people who came together to support proposals for a second pier some hundreds of yards further south to improve the ability of sea-going ships to reach the main channel. The new pier was to include a promenade, a jetty, a tramway and a toll house as well as saloons, bazaars, floating baths and landing stages.

It was argued that the original pier, with all its improvements, was most unattractive as well as being inadequate for the people of Southport and its multitude of visitors. It was claimed that in 1866 the Lancashire and Yorkshire Railway had transported 800,000 people into and out of the town. To promote the idea of a second pier - the Alexandra it was to be called - a company was formed with a predicated capital of £50,000, to build a structure variously stated as having a proposed length of 1500 or 1700 yards. (In order to get a rough idea of what these sums of money mean for construction in the terms of the year 2000, it is necessary to multiply them by something like 100.)

Inevitably, the new project was opposed by the existing Pier Company on the grounds that it would bankrupt them and also that they were themselves proposing further substantial improvements to the original pier which their committee, meeting early in

1867, had approved specifically in order to compete with the Alexandra Pier proposal. Nevertheless, the new project was endorsed by the Board of Trade, but the necessary Parliamentary Bill was rejected by the House of Commons Committee in March 1867. No reasons were given but the committee did say that they had been influenced by the undertaking of the existing Pier Company to go ahead with its stated plan of improvements.

So in March 1868, the local *Southport Visiter* newspaper reported that the various improvements had been completed, including the raising and widening of the extension pier, the erection of a large platform and landing stages right out into the channel, extending now nearly a mile from the promenade, Thus, the paper added "providing a safe and convenient place for the embarkation and landing of passengers by sea". Elsewhere it was reported that a floating bath was also provided near the end of the pier. The *Visiter* reported the view of the Pier Company that the improved pier, which had necessitated the increase of capital to £49,000, would not yield as high a return as the original, but it would be popular enough to bring an adequate yield.

In view of what transpired only some ten years later, special note should be made of three particular aspects of the 1860's saga of the competitive piers. Early in 1867 a letter to the Visiter argued that in view of the importance to Southport of a good pier, the proposed Alexandra Pier should be allowed to proceed in order to settle the matter "once and for all". Secondly, the promoters of the Alexandra Pier project argued that Brighton and Blackpool already had two piers. Finally, nowhere in the debate was any suggestion made that the whole problem had been made more important or difficult by any movement of the sea away from the promenade. It was just the town which had grown – by 10,000 in ten years, in fact, in the North Meols area as a whole.

The improved pier of 1868 apparently satisfied the needs of the town for it remained virtually unchanged until the major fire of 1933. By 1900 the Southport fleet boasted a hundred vessels which trawled fish off the coast at Morecambe to the North coast of Wales. Passenger boat services operated over a wide area with a regular service between Preston, Lytham and Southport and including excursions and services of various kinds to ports from North Wales to Barrow.

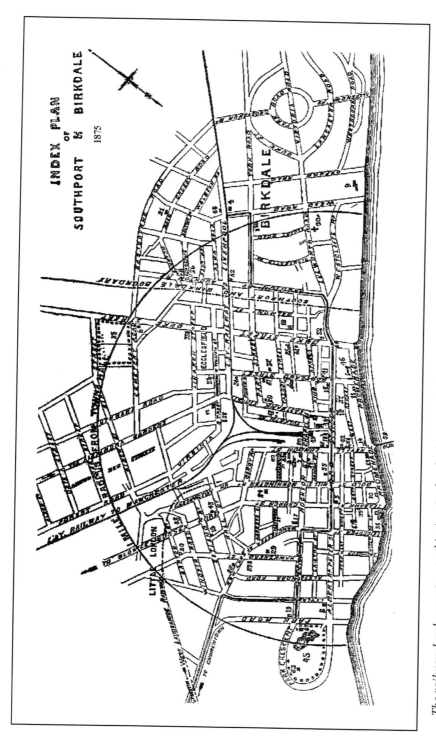

INDEX PLAN
OF
SOUTHPORT & BIRKDALE
1875

The railway development up to this time is clearly shown, with the Preston line under construction shown dotted to the left. To the right, the original plan for Birkdale Park is depicted; the actual layout is shown on the 1882 map – see page 50.

3
MATURITY: THE WINTER GARDENS

By the early 1870's then, the town of Southport, having multiplied fourfold in its own short railway age, was attaining maturity. Next to its precocious town hall, the foundation stone for the great Cambridge Hall was laid in 1872 by HRH Princess Mary of Cambridge (after efforts to persuade the Prince of Wales to come in conjunction with his visits to Wigan and Bolton had failed). The improved pier had turned out to be a great success with its toll income rising from £3,500 in 1863 to over £5,000 in 1873 and some £7,000 in 1874; the company was congratulated by the local newspaper (*The Visiter*) for having engaged the Hungarian Military Band for the 1874 season.

It was also reported that "numerous stately mansions are being erected around Hesketh Park and in Birkdale for our merchant princes". Very largely for their benefit, no doubt, in 1872 there was formed the new Literacy and Philosophical Society. Another sign of the times was that in 1874 was founded the Southport Improvement Association supported by the railway companies, the pier and the tramway companies, as well as by builders, tradesmen and the proprietors of various lodging houses. In May 1874 it was noted that a row of noble looking shops was replacing shanties on Lord Street.

In the same years, the town council was formulating plans for the provision of a public art gallery and a free public library, which were eventually donated by William Atkinson, a notable cotton baron, to be constructed along from the Cambridge Hall, with their foundation stone laid in 1874. William Atkinson came originally from Yorkshire and was successful as a partner in a company manufacturing coloured goods in silk, worsted and various dress materials. Later he became a partner in Tootal, Broadhurst & Lee, one of the major cotton textile companies, and he accumulated a substantial fortune. He came to Southport for his wife's health and made large donations to various churches before funding the Gallery and Library and paying for the illuminated clock for the Cambridge Hall.

The Gallery and Library were originally included in a single building but a few years later the Manchester and Liverpool Bank built another impressive building next door on the corner of Eastbank Street. In 1923 this was incorporated into the Library.

As if all this was not enough, early in 1873 was formed a company to build a Winter Gardens – with a capital of £30,000 - probably a more like £3m in 2000 money. This was an immense project for which the company acquired nearly 8 acres of land comprising the whole area from Lord Street to the Promenade bounded by Duke Street and Coronation Walk. Included in the plan were extensive gardens on both frontages, with £1,000 spent on plants, a band pavilion to accommodate 2,500 people and more, two great greenhouses, a grand terrace looking over the sea with a "sea breeze promenade", a carriage entrance and much else. At a lower level there was to be a major Aquarium with an extensive collection of fish from around the world.

The major objective of the company as stated in the official guide, was "to combine into a great and unique whole all that had been done in other seaside and watering places and to create a 'Winter Season in Southport'". The hope was expressed that "pleasure would be afforded to the ailing, the valetudinarians and all those seeking a brief retirement from the cares of business, especially in the great crystal hall". The local paper expressed the view that the gardens would complete the process of turning Southport into the Montpelier of the north.

Entry was by no means free or cheap. An annual subscription initially cost 2 guineas, subsequently reduced to 1½ guineas causing a dispute with the early subscribers; these sums roughly correspond to something in the range £100 to £200 in 2000 money. There is no mistaking the fact that this very significant project fitted well into the middle class, not to say upper class, pattern and tone of the town. There was very little in the Winter Gardens plan which seemed to constitute an attraction for "trippers" or the working class and their children in general. It was indeed later reported that each Saturday special trains were arranged to bring people from major centres of population to attend the frequent concerts, but the programmes featured in the local press revealed a generally serious and classical content.

In Southport outside the Winter Gardens there were some concessions to less sophisticated needs for amusement, specifically the "fairground" stalls and various entertainments situated near the pier. We must remember the statement made in 1867 by the promoters of a proposed new pier that some 800,000 people had been carried by train into and out of the town in 1866. In the spring of 1876 the *Visiter* reported that for Easter a great variety of trips were planned including 800 people from the Stalybridge Hurst Picnic Club, 800 from Middleton Junction, 1,000 Oddfellows from Barnsley Working Men's Club, and so on. A total of 8,000 to 9,000 visitors was expected on Good Friday – but in the event over 12,000 arrived and 8,000 of them paid 2d to go on the pier. To bring all these people to their nearest seaside town, the railway companies made eighty-four special trip arrangements for Good Friday followed by sixty-seven for Easter Monday.

However one defines the different social classes, there can be no doubt that the vast majority of this multitude of visitors belonged to the working class. What were the great attractions? For most people they were surely the sea, the beach (extolled by the local press as our "wide yellow sands") and, of course, the pier with its sea trips.

Such was the popularity of Southport that the West Lancashire Railway Company was trying to forge a new link to Preston and places further north. It was finding it hard to get Parliamentary approval for the right to join up with other lines in the Preston area, but in 1878 it completed its first 6 miles from Hesketh Bank to the recently created Hesketh Park, and by 1882 reached Longton and soon Preston itself.

The mid 1870s clearly represented the apogee of the opulent civic development of Southport with September 1874 perhaps the absolute pinnacle when the Cambridge Hall and the Winter Gardens were both opened with great festivities. In addition to Hesketh Park, where municipal provision had built on privately donated land, the Botanic Gardens and Museum were under construction as a purely private enterprise, as well as new Zoological Gardens on Scarisbrick New Road. The Library and the Art Gallery were under construction as a result of private beneficence. The Victoria Baths on the promenade had been rebuilt. New public gardens were created at Kew (near where the Meols Cop retail warehouse park stands today) and dancing became popular in their pavilion. A great new market hall on Eastbank Street opposite Chapel Street was being planned. The Prince of Wales hotel opened in 1876.

The dichotomy between this grandiose accumulation of provision for the well-to-do citizens of Southport and basic world of the "trippers" was epitomised in the discussions about the Southport Improvement Bill promoted by the Town Council in 1876 in order to secure approval for borrowing £410,000 for a number of projects including the extension of the gasworks, the lengthening of the promenade at both ends and various street improvements. A very vocal group of local people opposed the Bill partly because some of the projects were mainly for the benefit of trippers – said to constitute a problem "getting worse" year by year, but this group were heavily outnumbered.

Complaints about the trippers surfaced from time to time. The throng of 80,000 visitors in Whit week of 1877 clearly tended to swamp parts of the town, especially the promenade. The amusements located near the pier entrance constituted, said one local resident, something like a fairground. A father took his daughter for a walk on a Sunday evening along the promenade and pronounced it unsuitable for ladies at that time.

Yet the business brought by the trippers had clearly become important to the town. An outbreak of smallpox in 1876 damaged Southport's reputation, a fact which, coupled with the severe trade depression at the time, substantially reduced the number of visitors from the industrial towns and the amount which they spent. By February 1877 the local newspaper was reporting depression among hoteliers and shopkeepers, and a generally bad state in the town to the point that the Improvement Society was being urged to do something about the stagnation, including much better publicity around the country and even improved facilities for trippers.

The Winter Gardens was not doing well and was clearly searching for ways in which to improve revenue including the construction of a skating rink. The management was being criticised from all sides for "dumbing down" the music, turning the Concert Hall into a Music Hall, for instance, and for applying for a theatre licence. It is difficult to avoid the feeling that the management was trying to popularise the Gardens even to the extent of attracting more of the trippers.

So as Southport entered the last quarter of the century, having mushroomed astonishingly in the previous quarter, it had become extremely popular to two classes of people at the opposite ends of the social spectrum.

On the one hand, it had become a favourite place to live for the owners and senior managers of the cotton textile industry, as well as of other businesses, including the successors to the slave trade merchants from Liverpool. On the other hand, it was the most attractive and convenient place to visit – far more so than Blackpool

– for many thousands of people who did the hard work in the factories for these same and similar well-to-do local residents. There were obvious clashes of interest between the permanent and the temporary residents of the town, which were reflected in continuing disputes about investment in public and entertainment facilities. Yet the interests of all these people were to some extent bound together since fluctuations in the number and prosperity of the visitors had significant impact on the wealth of some of the business people and hence on the wealth of the town. The national trade depression of the 1870s clearly depressed business in Southport.

The worlds of the two classes of people were most strikingly positioned face to face on the promenade and particularly in and around the Winter Gardens the ornate frontage of which impressively dominated the view from the south end of the beach. Within its rooms there was an uneasy battle between two cultures. Outside, the smartly dressed Victorian promenaders overlooked the plebeian families on the sandy beach, with its donkeys and fairground entertainments. Although fluctuations of national trade could disturb the comfortable but divided scene, on the whole it seemed a stable prospect of "live and let live" at risk mainly of a very occasional stormy blast from nature or the economy.

Yet within six years of the opening of the Winter Gardens a meeting of local businessmen was considering a plan to build a new railway from a new station alongside the Gardens on Lord Street, taking in part of the Gardens' site and driving a track straight out seaward for a quarter of a mile before looping round to the south and running close to the foreshore where the coastal road now runs. How did this come about? We shall shortly begin to unravel the mystery.

MID-VICTORIAN
SPLENDOUR

Municipal Buildings 1875. The Town Hall (1854) and Cambridge Hall (1874) are shown with the site of the Library and Art Gallery alongside, occupied by a row of modest terrace houses.

Library and Art Gallery (1878). Both functions were combined in the one building donated by William Atkinson.

A bank was built a few years later further south and was incorporated into the Library in 1923.

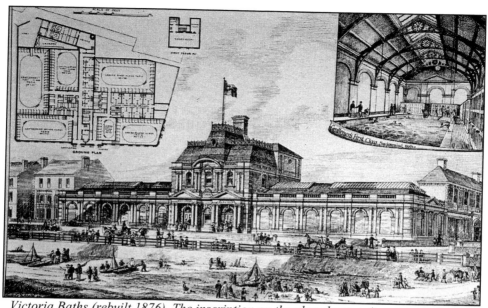

Victoria Baths (rebuilt 1876). The inscription on the plan shows quite separate Ladies and Gentlemen's entrances and accommodation each with first and second class. Gentlemen were also accorded a separate cold bath, all others being 'tepid'.

Market Hall on Eastbank Street (1876). The entrance to Chapel Street is on the right directly opposite the Market Hall which was burnt down in 1913 and eventually replaced by much smaller accommodation to the rear.

Victoria Hotel. Originally opened in 1842 as a modest hotel on the corner of the Promenade and Nevill Street, greatly enlarged in Victorian period. Finally demolished in 1971 to make way for existing typically gaunt 1970s blocks of flats.

Prince of Wales Hotel 1876. A 2001 picture but the hotel was little changed save for an extension.

Botanic Gardens Conservatory in Churchtown 1870s. This magnificent structure somewhat overshadowed the modest museum building.

Queen's Hotel. Open in 1866. Derelict in 2001 but being prepared for refurbishment as apartments. Unchanged frontage is prime example of mid-Victorian resort hotel.

Palace Hotel. The original block to the right was built in 1866. The extension block to the left was added in 1881 when the hotel became a hydropathic establishment.

Winter Gardens, 1874. Pavilion to left and Conservatory (Winter Gardens) to right. Note sea and beach in front below.

4
CATASTROPHE ON THE BEACH

On the 5th of March 1878 the local *Visiter*, seemingly out of the blue, published a very long leading article complaining that the promenade between the pier and Duke Street was, despite the recent expenditure by the council of substantial amounts of money, in a frightful condition. This phenomenon appeared, not surprisingly, to be connected with the fact that the beach in the area was a dismal swamp, not at all golden or fit to walk or ride on. It appeared to be a receptacle for bodies of dead dogs, garbage and stale fish, causing it to be evil smelling. After remarking that the sea and the shore had always been, and remained, vital to Southport, the paper explained that "the sea is deserting us more and more to the south west of the pier and running in more to the north-east".

Although this was the first occasion on which the *Visiter* had featured this dereliction of the south beach it reported that a plan had already been developed by two local men to remedy the catastrophe. It involved building a "circular" wall beginning at the promenade a short distance to the south-west of the pier, running 500 yards out from the promenade and curving back in again to terminate at the bottom of Duke Street. Some 66 acres would be enclosed embracing all the foreshore which was now so objectionable. The whole area would become a pleasure ground and would include a kind of serpentine lake a mile long enclosing two islands. The total cost was estimated as £30,000.

In the correspondence columns of the *Visiter* and at public meetings, the plan received wide support. Clearly the detail was modified over the years of discussion and planning but the south marine lake eventually created clearly bore considerable resemblance to the plan as described in the newspaper. However, even the first small lake did not open until 1887 - a gestation period of nine years. Before we look into what happened during this period, a few reflections seem to be in order.

In the first place we must note just where the catastrophe happened - right in front of the Winter Gardens, the sea front showpiece of Southport so recently and proudly constructed, precisely the area where the well-to-do residents and the more lowly trippers were most conspicuously juxtaposed. The foreshore so devastated was almost exactly alongside the original promenade, soon destined after much continuing debate to be extended north-wards. In other words it was at the very heart of the seaside at-traction of the town.

The second question is – how long had the deterioration been proceeding before the local newspaper brought itself to feature it? Obviously with a foreshore so flat as that at Southport there must have been some quite extended periods of lower tides when the top of the beach was not covered even at high tide, a problem en-countered in many places, so it is reasonable to believe that the extent of the problem was not detected for many months, a year or two even, and of course enough time had elapsed for a quite sophisticated plan to be developed to remedy it. It is hardly possi-ble that there had been no sign of trouble in 1877 or even 1876. Certainly there was nothing in local reports at the time the Winter Gardens was opened in 1874 to suggest the dire fate awaiting the pleasant and maturing resort.

There had been a regular joke about "seaside without the sea", clearly the great distance the sea retreated at low tide eventually extended nearly a mile to achieve a reasonable minimum depth. In this respect it was probably little different from Blackpool at the time and since. But of course this is not so unfortunate if the high tide does approach the promenade. Now, however, in 1878 it seems that sea bound trippers needed to walk three-eighths of a mile to reach the water even at high tide – although for the time being they could proceed more easily to the north end beyond the pier. Even so, the whole area bordering on the beach must have been greatly depressed by the forlorn and noisome aspect over such a vast area. Owners of substantial houses and hoteliers were particularly disturbed.

There is inevitably one major issue, which must have come to the minds of local people in 1878. Why and why here? We will consider this question at a later stage when account can also be taken of even greater upheavals of the beach over the years.

In the meantime we can begin to consider the impact of the im-mediate devastation on the attractions of the town for visitors. There is considerable difficulty in detecting significant changes in the number of trippers and in any event there were other factors involved, particularly "hard times" in the industrial area of Lancashire. This was after all the period of the Great Depression. However, some contemporary estimates of figures may serve as a benchmark for the future as well as an indication of the interests of the visitors.

The *Visiter* regularly published quite full reports of the Easter and Whitsun weekends. For Good Friday 1878 it noted that "hard times" had had a negative effect on the number of special trains chartered, but the resort was still crowded. A good high tide (presumably to the north of the pier) had ensured that Southport did not appear to be the seaside without the sea, and swings flourished near the Convalescent Hospital – at the north end by Seabank Road. There had been 8,000 visitors to the Winter Gardens.

The paper noted in passing that increasing competition was coming from Blackpool which had done much in the last two years to improve its attractions, leading to the opening of its Winter Gardens in July 1878. But Blackpool was still much smaller than Southport in this period – and suffered, so it was said, from bad smells!

The report for Whit Monday 1878 blamed the current cotton industry strike for the reduction in visitors from 1877, down, it was said, from 15,000 to 10,000 to 11,000. The beach was not very busy but 8,000 people paid to enter the Winter Gardens and the Botanic Gardens entertained 7,000 compared with 6,000 the previous year.

1879 appears to have been a mixed year. Good Friday was bright with a cold wind and saw "not so many trippers as usual". Particular comment was made that those who did come were almost all most respectable and well behaved. Although the circus could not perform because of restrictions on Good Friday, the Winter Gardens was thronged, and the roller skating rink was crowded. The new Art Gallery had 500 admissions and a church choir of thirty members sang glees. In the Cambridge Hall a Welsh tea party attracted 500 people. The swimming baths were also popular. At the new Glaciarum in the town an ice skating match was staged before the public had their turn.

For Whitsun the report was even more up-beat with some 16,000 visitors on the Monday. It was said that although times were still hard, not so much had been said about bad trade as in the previous two years. Again tributes were paid to the sober and orderly conduct of the visitors. A further encouragement was that the railway companies had promised that from July they would provide direct communications to the Midland Counties and London. Already people came from far and wide. Among the long list of towns from which special excursions came at Easter and Whitsun were Leeds, Bradford, Halifax, Dewsbury, Wakefield and Barnsley as well as many Lancashire towns and even Shrewsbury.

Clearly, the great flood of visitors from around the north of England and elsewhere had not so far been noticeably reduced by the putrid mess on the main beach. Of course the north beach was still in good shape for the many families with children for whom the real seaside was particularly attractive. What is most striking, moreover, is the great variety of interests displayed by the tourists in what Southport had to offer. Most of them seemed to visit the Winter Gardens and a half or more paid to go on the pier and/or found their way to the Botanic Gardens. Even 500 were admitted to the new Art Gallery on Good Friday. Almost everyone was well behaved. Even the few young men who insulted girls at the pier entrance on Guy Fawkes evening in 1878 were probably locals.

All this adds up to a picture quite at odds with the contemptuous remarks by some local notables about "trippers" reported from time to time and repeated in some local history books. What appears from the contemporary accounts is a vision of vast crowds of working people, well-behaved and with a variety of surprisingly sophisticated interests, enjoying the facilities originally provided by and for the comfortably-off residents of this newly matured and well-endowed resort as well as the basic attractions of the seaside.

A remarkable commonalty of interests and enjoyable pursuits is revealed between the effective representatives of the employers and the employed, as surprising as the enormous attendance at the Great Exhibition of 1851 had been to the authorities who feared even that the assembly of so many working class people would lead to revolutionary riots. The lower orders of the Victorian period seem to have been as respectable as their social superiors. Certainly they found great enjoyment in their occasional seaside relaxation from the long and severe years of toil in the factories and mines.

More than that, there was clearly a greater degree of economic commonalty between them than might be supposed from the on-going debate among the leaders of opinion in the town as to whether funds should be spent for the benefit of the trippers. The very fact that the local newspaper provided such regular reports on the holiday periods demonstrated that the tourist hordes brought much income to local businesses in an area which engendered very little in the way of its own added value in factories, workshops or mines. So the point which our story has reached in the middle of Queen Victoria's reign is the significant beginning of the on-going struggle of Southport to maintain and enhance its attractions, for well over a century, as the sea receded.

5
THE FIGHT BACK

The town's reaction to the catastrophe on the beach was interesting in being symptomatic of the period, although very surprising reviewed over a century later. Clearly, the muddy swamp stretching nearly a third of a mile from the promenade south of the pier required major public action both to remove the eyesore and to take advantage of the opportunity to create a pleasant replacement. But the mid-Victorian period was not attuned to major public initiatives funded by raising taxes, even on the wealthy citizens of a resort like Southport.

It must not be forgotten that, apart from the town hall complex, the major amenities of the town had been generally provided by private companies – the pier, the Botanic Gardens, the Winter Gardens – or gifted by private beneficence – the art gallery and the library. The railways, so vital to the town, were of course also the results of private enterprise, uncoordinated to the point of perversity.

The concept of public enterprise or provision even for the basic needs of the country for education was anathema in the age of rampant private capitalism. It was hard enough for the town council to find the money for a decent supply of water and gas plus an acceptable system of sewage disposal – witness the smallpox epidemic of 1876. So the idea of levying rates to fund the recovery and development of 50 to 100 acres (depending on how far south was considered) of devastated beach was hardly a starter. So obviously the question of private development of housing arose, only to be discarded not just because it would have meant accepting the isolation of the existing promenade, but also because the smoke from new houses would inevitably contaminate the existing comfortable dwellings along the promenade and beyond.

So there had to be another solution which did not cost the town unaffordable money. By 1880-81 there had been some recovery in national trade and even in Lancashire. The local press reported, however, that business in Southport was still poor even though other resorts were steaming ahead. The railways, both in their manic period and afterwards, had sought out every opportunity for potentially profitable business, or so one might have thought, bringing every likely seaside resort within access of people even through the middle of the country. Closer to home, Blackpool had long been discovered, as well as St Anne's and Morecambe.

Certainly this degree of competition in the north-west was of concern to Southport. Blackpool was the most important competitor with its wonderful long beach, away from the mud of the Ribble estuary. Before the railway came, it was, however, more remote from industrial Lancashire. Without the advantage of a major canal approaching within a few miles, like Southport, it had attracted a fair number of stagecoach excursions even before the end of the eighteenth century, but it had not blossomed into a well-to-do resort for cotton magnates and others Even when the first railway came to the Fylde in 1840, it went direct from Preston to Fleetwood, so Blackpool had to make do with a branch line from 1846 to 1874 and even then the through route was the slow coastal one.

So it was that by 1850, as the railway was beginning to make its tremendous impact on both resorts, there were already some 8,000 to 9,000 people living in the Greater Southport area, which was soon to build its impressive town hall, whereas Blackpool was hardly more than a large village, of barely more than 1,000 inhabitants. Of course, when the railway did come, both resorts expanded furiously, but Blackpool did not catch up in population until well into the twentieth century. But it was a very serious competitor for trippers and holidaymakers enjoying its golden mile of sands, a strip of pleasure-land with not much of a town behind it but no problem with a receding sea.

Indeed the very fact that Blackpool was a simple unsophisticated place seemed to constitute an added attraction for the factory workers of Lancashire compared to Southport with its development of amenities principally for the delight of its own well-to-do citizens. The railway companies soon appeared to appreciate this distinction and openly advertised "bathing excursions for the working classes" to Blackpool. These multitudes of customers developed, with a little help and encouragement, some of their own amusements, among which dancing, especially on the piers, became a particular favourite.

Even though Blackpool attracted in general a somewhat different class of visitor, it represented serious and quite local competition for Southport, along with other developing resorts, such as St Anne's which offered good beaches in quieter surroundings. It must be remembered that a high proportion of visitors of all classes were families with children, even and perhaps especially in this mid-Victorian period. What such visitors wanted, above all, for their seaside holidays were good beaches and close convenient seas.

This was the pre-eminent consideration which the leaders of Southport were apparently unwilling to recognise. Contrariwise, they argued that the attractions of Southport were still so great that, if sufficient visitors could not be attracted from Lancashire in spite of the well-developed railway system, they should be drawn from a wider area, perhaps from the English midlands, or even eastern countries. The strong view developed that whilst the railway companies, in their uncoordinated expansion in Lancashire, provided good services to Manchester and Liverpool with a through route to Preston soon to be completed, they had failed to recognise the need and the opportunity to bring people from other areas and particularly to provide good connections to the midlands.

Thus it was that in 1880 two great public meetings were held in the Cambridge Hall, chaired by the Mayor, with the objective of persuading the railway companies to provide through routes to the midlands. Unanimous resolutions were passed, but the railway companies were unsurprisingly not very impressed.

Two possible routes were proposed, one via Wigan and the other and preferred alternative was by means of a new line going south to connect near Aintree through the Lancashire and Yorkshire railway to the network of the Cheshire Lines Committee which was itself organised to provide connections between the systems of several major railway companies. Local enthusiasm, some might say desperation, was so great that, in the absence of movement by the existing railway companies, a new company was formed by local businessmen, the Southport and Cheshire Lines Extension Company, to build the 18 miles of track to Aintree. Enough funds were soon raised to warrant the promotion of a Parliamentary Bill in 1881.

The *Visiter* report of the discussion in the House of Lords Committee on the Bill was both amusing and very relevant. One peer commented that the trouble with Southport was that it did not offer the same attractions a such as Blackpool, Lytham (sic) and Morecambe. Was it true, he asked the proposers, that one had to take a tram halfway at least to reach the sea? He understood that during the spring tides it was a distance of 1600 to 1700 yards from the promenade to the sea at low tide.

This was hitting the nail on the head with a vengeance. Clearly, some detached people were clear headed enough to appreciate the real problem and to understand how optimistic, foolhardy even, the new venture was.

There were, of course, objections, both from the Lancashire and Yorkshire Railway and also from local residents in Birkdale about running a railway along the foreshore in front of their houses. There were obvious difficulties about bringing the line right up to the partly developed area adjacent to the end of Lord Street. Finally in 1881, Parliament approved the new line, but only up to the Palace Hotel in Birkdale, stopping short of the principal local problem area.

The huge luxury Palace Hotel had been built in lonely isolation in 1866 parallel to the shore and quite close to the beach, an almost incredible act of confidence at a time when the nearest railway station at Birkdale was over a quarter of a mile away. Like the rest of the wider resort, it suffered when the sea departed in the mid-1870s and by 1881 it was in such financial difficulty that it was transmuted into a hydropathic establishment, building a large extra wing in the process.

It is significant that representatives of the hotel company as well as of the nearby luxury Birkdale Park estate were among the leading promoters of the new railway line with a station on the hotel's doorstep. Yet the prospect of the new transport facility was not sufficient to change the prospects of the hotel radically.

A little further towards Southport, along Westcliff Road, a dozen great houses or mansions had also been built in the mid-Victorian period with their broad grounds running at the rear down to the cliff edge and the beach along what is now Rotten Row. Not surprisingly, the owners of these striking residences were as dismayed as anyone else at the replacement of the sea-washed beach by a noisome stretch of mud at the bottom of their gardens which was hardly regarded by most of them as an acceptable price to pay for a railway and its station close by. However, one or two of them turned out to be strong supporters of the railway, presumably because of their business interests in Birkdale Park and the Winter Gardens.

The railway solution proposed by the 1881 Act was inevitably quite unsatisfactory to the promoters of the project since they would have had to provide horse-drawn carriages to bring passen-

Mansion on Westcliff Road. One the typical Victorian mansions, with its grounds backing on to the cliff, being converted to apartments in 2001.

gers from Birkdale to Southport and back again. So in 1882 another Bill was successfully submitted to obtain approval to bring the line right up to Lord Street. Throughout this campaign, the Winter Gardens Company was not only supportive but also fully involved in the business venture. So much was this so that the company actually agreed that a large slice of their site should be surrendered, so that the line could have its terminus on Lord Street not far from Duke Street. Enthusiasm? - Certainly. Desperation? - Probably.

The ironic fact is that the final solution to the problem of bringing the train to Lord Street without major destruction of, or interference with, existing property was to take advantage of the basic problem of Southport itself. Between Birkdale and Southport pier the sea had receded to the extent that the line could be taken seawards in an arc from Birkdale just wide enough so that it could come finally at right angles under the promenade into the terminus on Lord Street itself. What miracle of imagination to make such a virtue of necessity! Even if it did mean surrendering part of the Winter Gardens which had opened with much acclaim and high hopes only eight years previously.

From the point of view of the town council, this was a wonderful plan since the new Railway Company was to provide a fair part of the resources to recover the devastated beach. The railway embankment was to be protected closely by a new promenade on the seaward side roughly along the line now followed by the Esplanade (where the Park and Ride entrance opens), reaching the old promenade opposite Coronation Walk. The land thus enclosed to the south would later become Victoria Park, future site of the Flower Show. The remaining foreshore to the north up to the pier would be turned into a garden near the promenade with a small marine lake of some six acres towards the sea, but without any protection for the time being.

So, with one bound Southport had freed itself from the bonds imposed by its twin problems, one real i.e. the receding sea and the other hypothetical i.e. the inadequate railway system? Well, no. To take the latter first, the new line did not connect with any new significant centres of population in the North-west, but only provided a somewhat tenuous link to places further South-east including the midlands. In any event it was always going to have to contend with the real problem of the disappearing sea which was due to get worse.

The year 1882, in which the new railway line was approved by Parliament, saw the belated completion of the West Lancs line to Preston via Longton. Both this line to the north and the Cheshire Lines Extension to the south which opened in 1884 were always going to struggle, given Southport's new endemic problem. Within a few years the sea had receded further and the north shore was also affected. So the marine lake was greatly expanded with a huge extension to the north being dug by 1892, making a total lake of 41 acres, which meant that a real alternative to the sea was beginning to emerge. A small area of sand had been left for children between the gardens and the southern marine lake, so adding to the creation of an artificial seaside.

Well seaward of the enlarged lake a new marine drive crossing under the north of the pier before turning inland was constructed by 1895, clearly taking account of the further movement of the ocean – the newly enclosed space became known as the Lagoon. But the whole area around Southport, including the seaward side, is so flat that not only does a few feet difference in sea level make

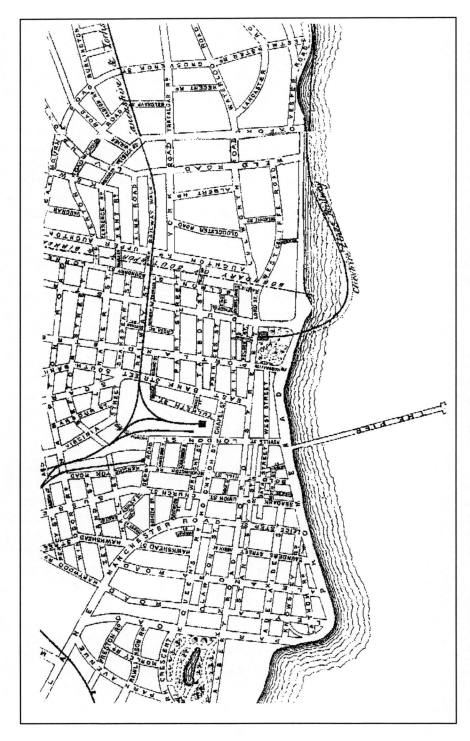

Map of Western Southport 1882. Note the sea is still extending in a bay towards Albert Road on the left. However, the dating of the movement of the beach is suspect because the Cheshire Lines Railway is shown running out to sea.

a great difference in tide limits, but an occasional very high tide, particularly when coupled with a storm, can go right over sea defences which normally seem more than adequate. This happened soon after the Lagoon was formed so that it was flooded, and the subsequent violent outflow of water along a narrow channel severely damaged the pier.

Even in the early 1880's when the sea had receded, a very occasional high tide would splash over the old promenade, a rare spectacle much enjoyed by crowds gathered on the pier. It also enabled the local newspaper to comment that Southport had not really lost the sea. This phenomenon also explains why in the late twentieth and early twenty-first century a new magnificent sea-wall has been constructed to protect the marine drive and everything to the east from one Park and Ride facility to the other, and so enable massive new leisure development to proceed.

According to R. Kay Greswell's 1953 book, *Sandy Shores in South Lancashire*, the nineteenth century was not a period when the general sea level of the Irish Sea was falling. Indeed, even in the twenty-first century, Blackpool still has its beach in much the same form. South of Birkdale the coastline has not changed much and even St Anne's is in reasonably good shape, although the sea rarely washes its sandy beach, now rather spoiled by mud. The real problem appears to have been centred on increasing silting of the Ribble estuary, which caused the authorities to take action to improve the water flow through the main channel quite near the Fylde Coast. This action further reduced the flow through the Pinfold channel and the 'Bog Hole' near Southport, resulting in a build up of silt and sand.

Early in the nineteenth century embankments had been constructed near Crossens and Marshside, which were 1¼ miles east of the coastline in 1845. By 1891 the latter had moved ¹/₃ to ½ mile further west. At Hesketh Bank by 1880 over a mile of new land had been reclaimed within fifty years. The process continued. A reliable witness reported that in 1909 there was a 60 feet depth of water at the end of the pier at low tide, but by 1924 this had reduced to 37 feet, and in 1928 the beach there was just dry at low water.

The new marine lake, even in its initial modest form, soon began to add new attractions to the foreshore area. A new opportunity was offered for rowing boats, and, reporting on the Easter weekend of 1890, the local newspaper commented that there were queues for the boats and urged the council to "do the same for the north beach". By Whitsun 1891 it was clear that the council had responded positively to this suggestion, since it was observed that the attraction for visitors of the existing marine lake was challenged by the interest shown in the work proceeding to the north of the pier. There were of course other attractions near the lake to the south - "switchbacks, swings, shooting galleries and small shows including George White's niggers".

There was also a completely uncovenanted pastime which developed during the severely cold weather early in 1891, when the marine lake, in spite of being composed entirely of salt water, froze hard enough to tempt some skaters to venture upon it. The suggestion was made that this activity would be both safer and more prolonged if the seawater was replaced by fresh water. The council, however, devised a quicker and cheaper alternative, i.e. to gently pour an inch or two of fresh water on top of the frozen seawater. Unfortunately the temperature rose a little the next day and a venturesome young man fell through the ice and was only rescued just in time after fifteen most distressing minutes.

The council's response to this near-tragedy was to half empty the lake so that its depth was only 30 inches, reducing the risk of drowning. This was just as well since the next day two people went through the ice. The *Visiter* recommended that the lake should be filled again to deter the adventurous. What a drama for the seaside!

In this 1890-91 period, the *Visiter* was still reporting the number of visitors coming to Southport by train at holiday weekends. At Easter 1890, the three railway companies brought some 25,000 on Friday and 38,000 on Monday on day excursions alone. Especially having regard to the fact that Easter was in March, these were phenomenal numbers to which all three-railway companies contributed substantially. On the Monday, the Cheshire Lines Extension's share was surprisingly high at 16,000, mainly from the greater Liverpool area, with some from Manchester. The Lancashire and Yorkshire company brought some 13,000 mainly from Manchester and Lancashire, whilst the West Lancs line carried nearly 8,000 from Preston and Blackburn. Inevitably the pattern between the three companies varied from one holiday period to another but Southport was clearly attracting a very large number of visitors.

To what extent this tourist business was attributable to the new railway lines is not clear, since it seems probable that they were mainly taking business from the old Lancashire and Yorkshire lines, partly by offering more convenient routes. There was certainly little sign that the Cheshire Lines were drawing many travellers from further afield. However, such visitors would have been expected to come for longer than a one day excursion and the *Visiter* was beginning to report modest numbers of visitors staying for weekends or even a week and ten days.

In considering the general tourist trade at that time, regard needs to be paid to the fact that in the last twenty years of the nineteenth century English working people were becoming substantially better off after a long period of distressingly slow increases in real wages as ample supplies of labour enabled factory owners engaged in increasingly competitive markets to hold wages down. The latter part of the century became known as the Great Depression mainly because of the increased trade competition in export markets particularly from Germany and the U.S.A. It was certainly a long period, hard to appreciate in the twenty-first century, of falling prices.

This great change in the economic situation was dominated by a huge increase in food supplies from the new continents opened up by overseas investment particularly in railways. In the 1880's the prices of cereal products, such as wheat for bread, fell to about half their 1860's levels; and meat prices fell by a quarter. Even with some cuts in wages and some increase in unemployment, the vast majority of people in jobs became significantly better off.

Of course, this increase in real wages did mean that working people had more spare money to spend on inessentials like holidays. So some increase in visitors to seaside resorts was natural, and such a trend could to some extent be expected to mask the difficulties made for Southport by the receding sea, but nothing could disguise the fact that the town was firmly in the grip of the most serious problem which a seaside resort could face. This was a bitter blow for the wealthy town which by the 1870's had seen a quarter of a century of tremendous expansion and the creation of the most astonishing array of social and cultural amenities which continued to attract both comfortably-off local residents and a multitude of visitors, all perhaps symbolised by the fact by 1880 the promenade had been progressively extended so that it ran from Duke Street to Park Road in the north where a wide arc led to the great expansion of mansions and large houses in the region of Hesketh Park. As we have earlier explained, the shape of the promenade in this area resulted from the fact that the sea did not recede from a deep bay until after 1880.

It has been reported by some local historians that Southport was not very interested in visitors or "trippers" as some people derisively called them. The town did not want to become another Blackpool, it was said. Such sentiments confuse different periods of history and indeed have little to do with history. As we have seen, there were some people who liked the town as a quiet and attractive place to live and did not want money spent on amenities which they saw mainly for the benefit of trippers. But these people were in a minority and lost out badly to the majority who recognised that the prosperity of the town had much to do with the money spent by visitors. Many local people had direct business interests in this expenditure and others recognised that its benefits were spread around the town.

Anyone who doubts that this was so has only to consider the enormous efforts made in response to the diminution of trade in the 1875 to 1885 period to restore it by attracting more visitors. Consider the great public meetings chaired by the Mayor to persuade the railway companies to improve their services. Consider the public willingness to see a railway installed along the near foreshore from the south and run into the end of Lord Street by curving out to sea and driving through the Winter Gardens site cutting off part of the skating rink – and to subscribe to it. Consider the fact that, once roused to the need, the council created new gardens, a great marine lake, a long marine drive and much else.

Contemporary evidence of the attitude of local people is afforded by a leading article in *The Visiter* for 4th August 1891 which first noted some of the special attractions for Bank Holiday visitors, such as the Cyclorama on the pier, "a grand series of pictures so realistic that the beholder is transfixed with astonishment", as well as performing fleas and Edison's photographic talking doll – and of course the Bands. At Kew Gardens there was to be a special band for dancing plus a grand gala and fireworks display in the evening. A bright note was also struck by a letter from a fisherman who claimed that for the past two years the sea had been returning!

The most striking aspect of *The Visiter's* article was a little homily on the general subject of the trippers. It noted first that the well-to-do people were hurrying off the continent or, as sportsmen, getting ready for the Scottish moors. Such privileged people who "lead a butterfly life" could take a month or many months if they liked to spend it in absolute idleness, but the mass of the people could only take very short breaks. The paper paid tribute to the Bank Holiday Act of twenty years earlier, which had brought about "a complete transformation of the life of the toiler" – it was now a national institution.

So what of the "trippers?" "They come here in their tens of thousands, jostle us in our streets, elbow us off the pavement and crumple us everywhere, but so good humouredly and so utterly unconcerned about it that it would really seem to be part of their amusement. We should be scrubby people indeed if we did not welcome them and take a delight in seeing their happy jolly faces. Next day it will be back to the grindstone for them in mill and workshop for many months. This will be their last opportunity of snatching a day's pleasure before the long dreary winter sets in".

No doubt this tolerant opinion was not shared by all the residents of Southport, but the fact that the local newspaper could venture such a public opinion is surely proof that hostility to the working class visitors was by no means universal. After all, in addition to their happy jolly faces – all 45,000 of them on August Monday 1891 – they brought money also to charm the local people.

If we jump ahead to the end of the century, to Easter 1900, we can try to assess how Southport's fortunes were progressing as a result of these attempts to counter its great handicap. The local newspaper reported that at Easter the weather was rather better than the previous year and on Good Friday the number of visitors was up from 10,750 to 12,350, and on Easter Monday from 30,000 to 32,500. The distribution between the railway companies was similar to that of ten years earlier with the arrivals at the Lord Street terminus of the Cheshire Lines Extension Railway coming almost entirely from the Liverpool area and Manchester. Clearly, however, the total numbers had fallen 63,000 over Easter 1890 to 43,000 in 1900. The town's problems were certainly not over. There was little sign of visitors being drawn from further afield.

Nature's die had certainly been cast and Southport could no longer compete with Blackpool on the latter's terms. Yet it had be-

The Opera House, 1890s. To the left is the terminus of the Cheshire Lines Railway and to the right the entrance to the Winter Gardens.

come a very substantial resort, having grown in the half century of its railway age from some 9,000 people in its total local area to 64,000, an amazing transformation in well under a lifetime. In order to succeed in the new century it needed to consolidate and enhance its many attractions away from the foreshore, recognising that its major problem could also offer a great new opportunity. The receding sea had presented the community with a great expanse of extra land. The crucial question would be what would it do with it?

Before we leave the nineteenth century, it is most interesting to note one final addition to the town's great entertainment attractions away from the sea as the result of an amazing act of confidence or even defiance. The Winter Gardens Company had in the 1880-84 years promoted and financially supported the creation of the Cheshire Lines Extension Railway, sacrificing part of its site and part of its sea view, a hazardous investment to be sure. Only six years later, the company decided that its Pavilion did not offer enough scope for musical and other entertainments, so it built a great Opera House fronting on Lord Street, complete with all the facilities and trappings appropriate to such a prestigious establishment and costing £20,000 – more like £2 million in money of the year 2000. The Opera House was opened in September 1891 with a great fanfare.

It was highly commended in the local press as a facility which would enable shows to be staged as good as any in the country. With six shops on its frontage and a veranda extending several feet over the carriageway, it provided an open-air promenade for the "occupants of the best part of the house". Private boxes for four people would cost a guinea, stalls and dress circle seat 5 shillings, the pit 1 shilling and the gallery sixpence. The paper's conclusion was - "The theatre is so complete and so comfortable that it is a credit to the company, a credit to the architect who designed it and a credit to the town of which it is an ornament".

Was this to be a great hostage to fortune or the clear sign of the town's readiness to face the twentieth century? Who could say? No one could foresee that the new century would be very different from the old with its first half dominated by wars and economic depression, followed by a second half which saw rising prosperity diverted substantially into overseas holiday travel as the era of the train was overtaken by that of the car and the aeroplane until we began to run out of both road space and air space.

In the meantime we should not overlook the fact that the great upsurge of wealth in the whole area and its hinterland continued

Lord Street: Albany Buildings with Preston Bank. The Bank (later Midland Bank, then HSBC) on the left, was opened in 1889. Albany Gardens was built earlier in the 1880s.

after the mid-Victorian period to develop and to promote the growth of commercial business in the later decades of the century leading to the ongoing development of Lord Street where noble bank buildings in particular replaced older shops and houses. By far the majority of the attractive and diverse premises fronting on to Lord Street were constructed in the 1880s and 1890s; and the Scarisbrick Hotel was reconstructed.

Yet the new century certainly began most anxiously for Southport. In 1901 the Winter Gardens Company ceased business and was taken over. But that is to anticipate.

6
PRELUDE TO WAR

As the new century opened, Southport was in a twilight situation. On the one hand, it had developed a great array of cultural and entertainment centres as well as a host of churches, private schools and increasingly golf courses. Among the churches, the newly rebuilt Holy Trinity was perhaps the most impressive as it remains, magnificently floodlit after further major refurbishment, at the beginning of the new millennium. The trams were being electrified. Not long ago the town had acquired two new railways and an Opera house.

On the other hand, its population growth had seriously slowed in the last decade rising only by 7,000 in the town proper after going from 18,000 to 41,600 in the previous twenty years, as noted by *The Visiter* which went on to bemoan a number of indicators of stagnation.

Holy Trinity Church. As refurbished in 2000.

"The fair on the sea-front was decaying, half the promenaders could not spare the energy to descend into the north marine park, however plaintively the pierrots pleaded and the town's band played to a shy spare audience. Music could not charm the Conservatory full nor the latest Parisian success nor the gayest serio-comic shows

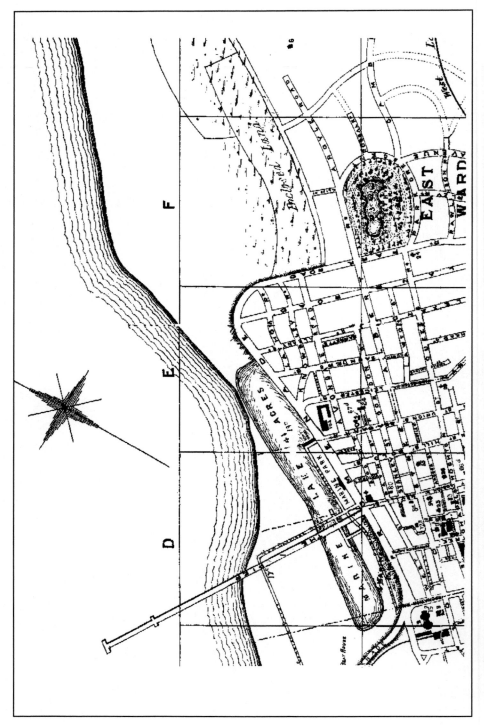

Map of North-western Southport 1901. Note that the Marine Lake has been extended to the north with the same width as the South Lake, and that the sea has receded far from Albert Road on the right.

Map of South-western Southport 1901. The recreation grounds enclosed by the railway, promenade and esplanade later became Victoria Park, site of the Flower Show.

from the London Halls pack the Pavilion. We are ennuied, languid. We have fallen on slack times."

The newspaper's proposed remedy for this doleful situation was the holding of a Great Exhibition much bigger and better than the one held in 1892 which was hardly a success. To start with, the Winter Gardens could offer a miniature Crystal Palace. Ambitiously organised, such an exhibition could earn a substantial immediate profit as well as drawing more and more visitors, and so more residents to the town. One thousand more householders were required to pay rates and spend more money. In any event, the welfare of the town and the prosperity of the Winter Gardens were closely linked. The latter sentiment was well founded, as we shall see. Indeed, early events were not helpful to the idea of a Great Exhibition, which did not happen.

On August Bank Holiday 1901 the weather was dull but 33,000 people came to the town (including 5,500 weekenders), 10,000 more than in the previous year. Of these a total of 6,000 attended the three performances of the Pierrots around the theatre in the North Marine Park. There was some suggestion that this show had damaged the business of other entertainment venues, especially as many people were able to watch it for free and did so, despite the lack of shelter from rain and sun. Should the council, which provided the Pierrots' show, be competing against the ratepayers, i.e. the private entertainment companies?

Of these, the Pier Company had been driven by a fire in 1897, causing £4,000 worth of damage, to build a great new Pavilion at the pier entrance, set back 60 feet to allow for a broader promenade. To finance this venture, the company issued a debenture for £30,000, a tremendous sum. This Pavilion, which opened on New Year's Day 1902, was to become the venue for many famous variety stars over a long period, Gracie Fields and George Formby among them. It accommodated 1,500 people and was lit by electricity, with a gas system in reserve!

While it was being built, the local paper reprinted an article from a Bournemouth journal by a citizen of that town who had visited Southport to investigate the title ascribed to it in some quarters of the "Bournemouth of the North". This writer explained that his town was gifted by Nature but Southport had to produce its attractions by Art. But its sea was steadily receding and the pier was hardly usable by sea-going boats at low tide; even when

Pier and Marine Drive. Early 1900s. The new Pavilion was opened in 1902.

they got to sea their progress was impeded by sandbanks. Southport had a good promenade which Bournemouth so far lacked, but the latter's central gardens far outweighed the quite pleasant Southport features and even its well-laid out boulevards.

The Southport pier was said not to be too popular with its 2d toll (and 2d more to go on the tram) a deterrent, although the new Pavilion would help. The article noted that while the day-tripper was not unknown in Southport his welcome was not of the heartiest! The writer's conclusion was that, even allowing for Southport's safe boating on the lake, for pleasure on the sea or by the sea Bournemouth had superior claims as well as greater inland attractions.

The two seaside towns did have some similarities compared at least with Blackpool. By 1911 both had many fewer lodging-house keepers in relation to the total number of households i.e. under 10% compared to over 30% in Blackpool. Both had nearly twice as many domestic servants in relation to their population as Blackpool. In short, they were both places where more well-to-do people came to live – including retiring – than Blackpool. The huge figures for day trippers to Southport on bank holiday week-ends indicate that comparatively few of its visitors came to stay even over one night. Certainly Bournemouth seemed to have many more hotels.

It could be argued that the comparative lack of hotels in Southport was responsible for the lower number of "stayers" on holiday. More likely it was the lack of demand which was responsible, the result of the loss of the convenient and attractive beach. We know that the Palace Hotel suffered. The town had a populous hinterland within easy distance by train and so was attractive to day trippers, but families with young children were not so likely to come for their week's holiday. Personal contacts in the midlands and Lancashire in the 1930s and 1950s confirm that Southport was not on most families' short list for summer holidays because it was not regarded as a real seaside place.

Another sign of the times in 1901 was the sale of the Cheshire Lines Extension Company to the Lancashire and Yorkshire Railway, which had already acquired the West Lancs line to Preston, for £332,900 of debenture stock, a surprisingly high figure. Was this just simple consolidation or monopolisation? Who knows?

The unmistakable signs of difficulties in the entertainment and leisure business in Southport were soon to have striking confirmation. The Winter Gardens was clearly having serious problems, probably exacerbated by the determination of the Pier Company to build its attractive new Pavilion. Late in 1901 the company, which had developed the magnificent Gardens, invested in the Cheshire Lines Extension Railway and only ten years earlier built a fine Opera House, was wound up. The complex was taken over by North Marine Entertainments which added new roller and ice skating rinks and turned the sunken garden next to the promenade into a boating lake and a switchback railway.

In 1905 the property was taken over by a new Southport and Winter Gardens Company which reconstituted the Pavilion as the Albert Hall Palace of Varieties. By 1910 it was The Empire for variety and picture shows and in 1913 was transformed into a "luxurious first class picture theatre", becoming the Scala, the first "talking" cinema in the area. But for the Winter Gardens it was really downhill all the way until the Opera House was destroyed by fire in 1929 and the whole complex soon demolished apart from the Scala which by then was in a separate building.

By 1910 it was clear that Southport was in considerable difficulty. A town councillor complained that it was going backwards, reflecting the lack of action on the part of the council. There was a need for a constructive policy embracing the development of Lord Street, the provision of winter attractions and the widening of

Nevill Street. The main approach to "the front" remained a disgrace to the town. A clear symptom of decline was "the gradual and persistent reduction of better class visitors".

There were other signs of the times in this pre-war period. Advertisements began to appear in the local press for excursions from Southport to destinations all around England, including the south coast, as well as to Scotland and Ireland. It was said to be the era of flats, some of which were developing at the north end of the promenade. There was a proposal to encase the railway in the Birkdale area and build a promenade on top, even as far as Ainsdale, but this did not happen.

Yet there were some positive signs. At Easter 1910, even though it fell in March, there was a large stream of visitors beginning on Thursday afternoon and the total for the holiday on the Lancashire and Yorkshire Railway system was reported to be 17,000 higher than in the previous year, although industrial depression was reducing their expenditure per person. The fair ground, which had been moved to the south end of the lake, was very popular. There was a nursery on the seashore, patronised by 114 babies on one day. All the visitors were reported to be very orderly.

At Whitsun, too, there were great crowds enjoying good weather. Paddling was popular at the south end of the lake. The usual colourful dress was missing because of the recent death of King Edward VII. There were good attendances at three band concerts on Lord Street. Boating on the lake was so popular that there were many capsizes, but the water was safely shallow. One rotund mother was heard to say to her son in the water – "Never mind lad, its salty water so tha can't catch cold"!

The new Winter Gardens company was apparently encouraged to try to recover its palmy days. To the Opera House, Sir Herbert Beerbohm Tree brought his company from His Majesty's theatre in London to perform *Trilby* and other plays. In the Empire there were two variety performances each evening. Other shows were on offer in the Pier Pavilion, at the Pier Head and in the Pavilion in the Winter Gardens.

There were some positive developments. Significant industry had come at last to the area in the shape of the Vulcan Motor works and in 1905 the status of the town was raised to county borough status followed by merger with Birkdale in 1912 in which connection it was being obliged to treat its sewage properly.

Picture Palace. This 2001 picture shows the only surviving cinema in Southport which claims to be the oldest survivor in the North-West. It was opened in 1911, the second in the town.

By 1913 there were four "picture palaces" including one at Birkdale – for black and white silent films of course and they won the battle to open on Sundays. Broadbents in Chapel Street was advertising itself boldly as the BARGAIN MECCA OF THE SHOPPING WORLD. The Lancashire and Yorkshire Railway was giving up its proposal to build a new line from Kew Gardens station to Ainsdale to join up with its Liverpool line to provide through services from the growing districts of Hesketh Park, Churchtown and Meols Cop, avoiding Chapel Street. The corporation was defeated in Parliament on its proposal to run trackless trams to give trippers a joy ride on the sea front. However, other attractions were appealing; one advertisement read –

FORESHORE
PLACE TO SPEND HAPPY HOLIDAY
FIGURE 8 RAILWAY – RIVER CAVES
HELTER SKELTER AND ESCALATOR
ALL BRILLIANTLY LIT AT NIGHT

Palladium Cinema. Opened in 1913, the third cinema in the town; finally burnt down in 1929 and rebuilt soon after. The black and white buildings were built in the late nineteenth century and still stand.

Bank Holidays continued to attract the crowds – 61,900 on August Monday, said to be more than the previous year with the fair and boating very popular and the military band well supported in the gardens.

Yet foreign travel was becoming more popular. Scarcely a European resort was not patronised by some working class people travelling by train, whilst middle class people were covering three or four countries, some now by motor car.

The corporation was reacting to the call for improvements in the town with a grand plan to spend the very large sum of £110,000 – close to £10m in twenty-first century money. This project was possible because other liabilities had been reduced and an annual profit of £15,000 was being made on municipal undertakings, including the provision of gas and electricity, despite a loss on tramways.

Of the total amount, £13,000 was spent on increasing and improving the gardens at the south end of the lake up to the Esplanade, incorporating three bowling greens and a "beautiful terrace" overlooking the lake. There were 100 boats on the lakes and a variety of amusements for children. The south promenade was being doubled in width and the footpaths and gardens were being improved. A children's paddling pool was to be created at the edge of

Paddling pool, early twentieth century. A corner of the North Marine Lake.

the north marine lake near the Marine Bridge.

To cap it all, Queen Victoria's statue was re-erected at the foot of Nevill Street where it still stands today.

Clearly this great panoply of improvements merited a very special opening, so King George V and his Queen duly arrived on 8th July 1913 and the extended gardens at the south end of the lake became the King's Gardens. There were, of course, joyful celebrations with bands playing, regattas, swimming races and so on, completed by a water carnival on the south lake. The King and Queen did not see it all, by any means. After an hour or two in and around the Cambridge Hall, witnessing a parade, listening to the band and meeting a host of celebrities, the King simply pressed an electric button to open the King's Gardens – modern miracle! The royal carriage took a short tour of part of Lord Street and the promenade before leaving via Churchtown for Preston.

So it seems that Southport, with its enlarged population of some 80,000 people, covering an area of some 7 x 1½ miles, ended the long period of peace, if not of undimmed prosperity, in triumphant mood. Its well-to-do citizens had certainly created for themselves a most attractive place to live with many amenities of culture and entertainment in a pleasant environment. It was also still a magnet for short-stay trippers from its industrial hinterland although obliged to relinquish its claim to be a seaside resort like

King's Gardens. Opened by King George V in 1913.

Blackpool, St Anne's or Morecambe.

A strange dichotomy of cultural taste had emerged which could not be wholly attributed to its dominating upper middle class citizens and its working class trippers, for the latter could hardly keep its picture palaces and variety shows going all year round check-by-jowl with its classical concerts and operas. In short, a most fascinating place, never quite knowing where it was going, especially in the thirty odd years since the sea left it. There remained much scope for the town to settle down and work out its future in growing maturity after its phenomenal adolescent growth from 9,000 to 80,000 in sixty odd years during which the movement of people had gone from the early wonder of rail travel to the beginnings of overseas holidays. Whatever may be said, enthusiastically, about the marvels of air travel and communications since the Second World War, the changes in people's lives were surely greater in the Victorian period.

It would be fascinating to conjecture how Southport would have progressed in its maturity in peace and progress. But both were to be shattered time and again in little over thirty years, so that nothing would be the same again.

Looking back, it is noteworthy how far the town had already moved from a basically private enterprise operation with many local people investing in it and the private landowners controlling development. As we have seen, the town's corporation had ventured further than most towns into municipal enterprise in tramways, gas and electricity, making profits which helped it to beautify the foreshore, as well as the town itself, to compensate for the depredations of nature, indeed making a virtue of necessity. Eventually, as the new century progressed much more of this virtue and this enterprise would become vital.

7
BETWEEN THE WARS

1914 was more of a watershed for Southport, as indeed for England, than 1900. It began a long period of immense disruption after the century of general peace and economic and political progress, albeit subjected to many ups and downs, since the Napoleonic wars. Of course the Great War was a tremendous waste not only of people but also of resources, a vast hiatus in the course of progress. It was followed closely by a severe international economic depression and then when recovery seemed to be on the way, by the return of sterling to the old gold standard. The resultant downward pressure on wages led to industrial strife culminating in the general strike of 1926. On Whit Monday of that year the number of 'trippers' to Southport fell to 21,000 from 47,000 in 1925.

Aerial view showing Cheshire Lines Railway, Pleasure Land and open air pool, 1920s. Note that the beach and the sea still came well up to the Esplanade and the Pool but seem already to have receded a long way in the north.

Three years later the Wall Street crash threw world business into chaos involving dire unemployment everywhere. From the mid-thirties in England recovery gradually strengthened, but in a few years the country was at war again.

War and economic depressions accelerated political changes which had begun earlier. In Britain the right to vote had gradually been extended during the nineteenth century first to the middle classes and finally in the twentieth century to everybody, except to women. As a degree of prosperity developed, working class people began to emerge from near-slavery in factories and mines. Children even began to go to school for a reasonable period instead of working. Trade Unions developed, particularly among skilled workers, and in turn promoted the Labour Party, which began to win seats in Parliament and, in the inter-war period to form Governments. Meanwhile a great Liberal Government took office in 1906 and introduced vital social reforms. Working people began to be given modest paid holidays and by the 1930s the local press in Southport was regularly publishing the dates of the Wakes Weeks of seventy or eighty Lancashire towns.

Gradually the political left began to infiltrate local government and although Southport, so far dominated by the business and professional elite, was never going to be governed from the left, more regard had to be paid to the needs of the working classes. During the war promises were made by the government for social improvement including "houses fit for heroes" so in 1925 the *Southport Visiter* was reporting favourably on various housing schemes which were making contributions to providing "houses for the people", a strikingly radical turn of phrase.

By 1926 municipal town planning was taking over from the great local landowners, whose estates were in any event being split up, and the town was being divided into zones for different densities of housing development. The poor were still to be kept apart from the rich, but at least their needs were beginning to be recognised.

Other long term factors were steadily changing the environment for Southport. These were not just the new technological factors like electricity and the internal combustion engine, although we should note in passing that the electrification of the Liverpool railway line from 1904 had raised the daily number of trains each way from forty to sixty-three in the summer with another twelve expresses stopping only at Birkdale – clearly commuting from

Southport to Merseyside had become common as well as tripping traffic in the reverse direction.

The vast increases in industrialisation in the nineteenth century, accompanied by similar increases in trade and shipping, had brought a multiplication of population in Southport's hinterland. Its closest city neighbour, Liverpool, had doubled from 375,000 in 1850 to some 750,000 in 1900 including Bootle. Manchester and its many sister (or daughter) industrial towns in Lancashire had grown similarly. It therefore seems clear enough that the self-styled "garden city" did not really have to look very far afield to garner its audience of admiring visitors or even more residents.

Thus, in spite of the prevailing unhelpful economic situation, soon after the war the town felt able, if not duty-bound in the interests of both residents and visitors, to resume the process of making moderate progress towards repairing the ravages inflicted by the departing sea or taking advantage of them, if you prefer. The war had most obviously caused a hiatus in the project of doing something more attractive with the lagoon, the unsightly remains of the beach enclosed by the marine drive which ran from the most seaward point of the esplanade, first for a few hundred yards towards the sea, then turning right to the north to go under the pier before turning right back to the promenade and constituting still today what is known as Marine Parade.

Just before the war a start had been made in filling the lagoon. By the early twenties this process had been completed and the recovered area was opened by the Prince of Wales, as Prince's Park of course. The town had done quite well really, to get the King to come first before the war and the Prince quite soon afterwards! The park was embellished by an arched colonnade the line of which can still be observed as a semicircle of concrete. A few years later an open air sea bathing pool was opened, towards the sea, which became extremely popular in good weather over many years until holidaymakers sought warmer water overseas.

These attractive improvements completed the out-of-doors embellishments of the marine lake and gardens area south of the pier. However, the sea was still retreating further and from 1923 the pier had been left so high and dry that commercial boat trips, even from its extremity, had to be abandoned for lack of water. By the 1930s the northern beach area was becoming drier as well and it was clear that a major new problem, or opportunity,

NEW OPEN AIR BATHS, SOUTHPORT.

Open air pool: aerial view.

needed to be addressed. Early in 1938 the council published a proposal hugely to expand the northern marine lake mainly towards the sea but also northwards, thus creating a total lake area of some 100 acres compared with the forty-one acres resulting from the expansion of the 1890s. The marine drive was to be extended around the new northern lake. This proposal was generally welcomed by the local press. It was noted that it would enable the sailing club to operate on a broad safe water area without the risks of sailing on the sea which was often hostile and forbidding and had sometimes virtually disappeared. It should be possible, one correspondent suggested, to run two regattas a year, foreseeing the annual twenty-four hour race.

But a project of this magnitude could not be finalised quickly. There had to be full opportunity for all shades of opinion to be consulted including those people who foresaw the need for more indoor leisure facilities, as well as to consider the financial problems. Already the coming war was beginning to cast its shadow in advance and there were some suggestions that the development should include provision of air-raid shelters. In fact the new war did start before anything was done. It would cause a hiatus just like the first great war, but much longer, very much longer.

In the meantime, however, the marine lake had been embel-

Open air pool: inside. Hugely popular!

lished by the council's building of the Floral Hall in 1932, with a plain exterior but with art deco enhancement in the interior. It included an auditorium to seat 1600 people and a front area of 900 square yards with a sprung floor for dancing. The Southport theatre would not be added for another forty years.

Another example of the uncertain atmosphere of the years of inter-war depression is the fact that the Botanic Gardens and Museum Company, which in the balmy days of the mid-1870s had shown a remarkable demonstration of wealthy local private enterprise, was declared bankrupt in 1932. The Museum's collection had to be sold by auction to pay the company's creditors. By 1937 in a somewhat more prosperous period, the Council was persuaded to restore and re-open the Gardens and Museum. After a new collection of exhibits was built up, the Museum re-opened as the first local municipal enterprise in this field.

The Opera House was not the only major place of entertainment to be burned down in 1929. The Palladium Cinema, built on Lord Street, on the site now occupied by Sainsburys, in 1913, the same year the great Market Hall succumbed to fire, was a "state of the art" luxury venue. It too perished in 1929. However, both these substantial losses were replaced, the Palladium in record speed in 1930, the Opera House on a more leisurely timescale by the

Floral Hall. Obviously very floral originally.

Garrick Theatre in 1932, an elegant building in the Italian Renaissance style with a foyer in the Egyptian style.

The Pier Pavilion had numbered George Robey and Charlie Chaplin amongst its star attractions. Flanagan and Allen apparently first sang 'Underneath the Arches' on its stage. By the 1930's, however, it was experiencing harder times and was renamed the Casino and subsequently leased to the Southport Repertory Company. But the Dramatic club, having occupied the

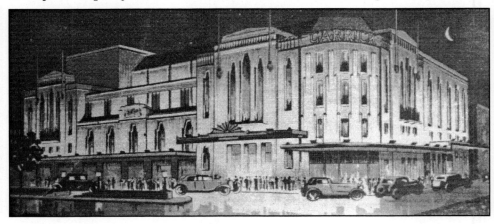

Garrick Theatre. In its original splendour.

Garrick Theatre for some years, was blessed with its own Little Theatre in 1937.

There was indeed great competition amongst the multitude of places of entertainment in the 1930's. By 1938 the local paper featured 14 major advertisements for theatres and cinemas and a new cinema was being built on Lord Street opposite the Garrick Theatre. Television was of course still a long way off but "wireless" programmes appeared in the press.

Early in the 1920's there had been improvements in Lord Street including the erection of the new war memorial and "artistic transformation" of the Municipal Gardens. Coronation Walk and Duke Street were widened and a few new buildings of some distinction appeared on Lord Street including a Palais de Danse and two fine bank buildings, one of which now houses Waterstone's, and the other, which was originally the National Westminster, has recently been a bar/restaurant called 'Quid Pro Quo', refurbished early in 2001 and re-named The Old Bank which was originally close to the Waterstone's building.

Most significantly, attention was drawn to the improvement of the approach roads: Lord Street West was widened and the first 1¼ miles of Preston New Road opened between Churchtown and Crossens. The era of the motor car was really beginning.

Indeed, it was reported that on Easter Saturday 1929 there were 20,000 to 30,000 cars in town which is hardly believable,

Garrick Theatre. As vandalised in the late twentieth century.

but obviously there were a lot and 2000 of them parked on the beach. On Easter Monday there were still many people coming by train, 80,000 it was said, and 169 children were looked after in the Excursionists' Day Nursery. At Whitsun there were car races on the beach to an audience of 100,000. Pleasure Land was always thronged.

By 1938 the picture had little changed with 50,000 visitors on Good Friday with 20,000 still coming by rail to the main LMS Station on Chapel Street but only 2000 to Lord Street mainly from Manchester, Stockport and Stalybridge. With

Quid Pro Quo. A 2001 picture of 1922 National Westminster Bank. The café bar was refurbished early in 2001 and reopened as The Old Bank, a title originally given to a bank further north along Lord Street.

electric trains running every five minutes from Merseyside on the Liverpool line, it was hardly surprising that the Cheshire Lines Extension railway was finding it even more difficult to survive. Of course it now had to cope with competition from buses and cars. The Formby by-pass opened in 1938 and there was hope of a dual carriageway to Preston in eighteenth months.

From all the reports it was evident that holiday tourist travel in Southport depended very heavily on the weather. With the great improvements in transport, potential visitors from many miles around could take last minute decisions about travelling. Few of them came long distances, and although the local hotels were usually booked at holiday weekends, their clients constituted only a modest proportion of the tens of thousands of tourists who thronged the foreshore and Lord Street, which by Easter 1938 was revelling in the "fairyland loveliness of illuminations".

A striking instance of the effect of the weather is that Whitsun 1937 in good weather and with Coronation decorations on display, a record 120,000 people came to the garden city, a figure reduced by about a third in poor weather in 1938 with the electric trains from Liverpool bringing 15,000 instead of 25,000. Yet those who came spent a lot of money.

Like the rest of the British people, the citizens of Southport had no doubt suffered to some extent as a result of the severe economic vicissitudes of the inter war period, but by 1938 they must have been reasonably prosperous. A few years earlier the Town Clerk had declared his confidence in the future of the garden city claiming that nearly all of its houses did in fact have gardens and that there no slums. On the other hand, it was true that many of the large middle classes houses nearer to the town centre were occupied by several families, an arrangement for which they were ill suited. In part, of course, this was because servants were becoming too expensive for the castles in the sand.

In any event, the town had come to terms with the fact that, without large changes which could not yet be contemplated, it could not compete as a family seaside resort with the likes of Blackpool, Morecambe and St Anne's, let alone places further south to which excursions were now widely offered. Yet despite the grievous loss of the Winter Gardens it had no problem in attracting a multitude of short term trippers from its populous close hinterland.

Indeed, the town could well have rested on the laurels of its improvements around the marine lake as well as its always blossoming Lord Street, but for the fact that the sea had already withdrawn further from the northern lake leaving an eyesore which could hardly be ignored. As we have noted, this huge blemish was going to remain for a long time. We shall have to discover how this great delay was allowed to happen as the new world of travel opportunities opened up in the second half of the century with dire implications for the real seaside resorts as well as for Southport.

8
POST WAR RECOVERY

The Second World War damaged the British economy to a much greater extent than the first, partly through the loss of overseas investments but also because of the neglect of virtually all kinds of maintenance and particularly as a result of the lack of investment in industry and social and civic assets such as schools, housing and civic buildings. On the other hand, in Britain and elsewhere the post-war economic recovery was much better managed so that there were no major depressions and by the mid-1950's a degree of prosperity had returned with unemployment very low. Soon Prime Minister Macmillan could tell the people that they had 'never had it so good.'

Nevertheless, the leeway in public investment took a long time to be made up; it was unrealistic to expect that new municipal ventures in a place like Southport would quickly be promoted, The effects of post-war austerity and the rise of motor cars were seen in the closure to passenger traffic in 1952 of the Cheshire Lines Extension Railway which had always struggled since it was opened.

It was the beginning of the age of television and there were signs of its impact on live theatre and although the two dramatic societies in the town continued to operate, the Garrick Theatre was sold in 1957 to the Essoldo cinema circuit. The cinema business continued to thrive until well into the 1960s although in 1966 the Grand became a casino. In 1959 there was even a spell of ballet at the Essoldo.

Not until the 1960s did the overseas holiday business really begin to take off and by 1959 the post-war recovery had matured, with high levels of employment and better wages, to the extent that Southport achieved something like its twentieth century apogee. *The Visiter* noted that people were generally working shorter hours and enjoying more leisure. Proposals for large blocks of luxury flats around Lord Street were appearing. A start was made on a sea embankment scheme around the north marine lake, which was still in its original form, no wider than the south lake, with the objective of preventing the lake silting up through its connection to the sea. Peter Pan's Playground on the seaward side of the north lake near the pier was opened with its small bathing lake and beach.

Peter Pan's Pool and Playground.

Pleasure Land was the beneficiary of a £50,000 development scheme by Helters Ltd to include an open air café on Marine Drive and a bridge over the 'fair' to the River Caves.

There was also a proposal for the Corporation, which had taken over the pier, to spend some £15,000 on additional covered accommodation, including a restaurant, at its seaward end, and there was much concern that the scheme was cut out of the budget for 1959-60, presumably because the local rate was going up from 15s 6d in the pound to 16s 9d even without the scheme. However, the Corporation continued to develop the plan until in June a fire severely damaged the buildings towards the seaward end of the pier, destroying the amusement arcade, café and Ships Cabin Bar, with total damage estimated at £50,000. The Corporation's response to this disaster was to prepare a new plan for the pier, to cost some £30,000 involving the provision of much more covered space by trebling the size of the bar, doubling the café and providing a temporary amusement arcade. The seaward end of the pier was to be shortened by several hundred yards – after all it was no use anyway for boats – so that its total length was a little over 1200 yards.

Before the fire, in mainly good weather, 40,000 people had paid for admission to the pier over four days at Easter. In June, in good weather on a non-holiday weekend, the sea bathing lake had its best season for thirty years with 11,000 people paying for admission on a Sunday and there were 13,000 cars parked on the beach. On August Bank Holiday (still at the beginning of the month) 38,000 deck chairs were hired out and the early demand for the Flower Show was a record.

The accommodation situation was revealing. In spite of low advance bookings at hotels for the summer holiday periods it was feared that for the bank holiday weekend there would be a shortage of modest accommodation and a special appeal was made for anyone with spare rooms to register with the council.

Thus the pattern of the town's tourist trade was reconfirmed. Yet the increased leisure time and higher wages of many people, together with their improved transport facilities, embracing buses and cars as well as trains, resulted in the tripper boom spreading to many weekends when the weather was good.

In 1960 the corporation at last felt able to pick up the plan proposed just before the war to fill the gap which had long developed to the seaward side of the north marine lake as the sea had receded further. The scheme finally adopted in April 1961 was to devote most of the further 90 acres reclaimed from the sea by the new embankment to the widening of the lake to pretty much the shape as it remains in 2001, although a modest further extension of its length to the north was added some years later. The total cost was estimated as £75,000 of which £15,000 was allocated for 1960-61 and the work would take two to two and a half years.

During the discussion of this plan, one councillor remarked that "When we walk along the foreshore all we can see is a watery waste, stagnation and breeding ground for insects carrying all sorts of diseases". Whatever the truth of the latter assertion this great improvement had taken a long time to be achieved, but the municipality could hardly carry all the blame.

There had indeed been some opposition even at the end, including that from people who had wanted to see more and more gardens with more leisure facilities. However, the cost of all this kind of extension to the existing open spaces around the lake would have been considerable with little income to defray high maintenance costs. The extended lake, on the other hand, would produce an estimated income of £10,000 a year including fees from two sailing clubs. It was forecast that 500 yachts could safely sail on it.

Some of the extra recovered land at the pier end was to be devoted to a children's beach and at the north end a special area was also to be arranged, with good sand cover, for mothers and children.

A somewhat amusing feature of all this great improvement to seaward was that a new sea road was being developed along the new embankment and progressively extended north and south. The corporation responded to criticisms of its bumpy surface by explaining that it was only temporary and would be replaced by a more permanent road when the foundations had been consolidated, perhaps in ten years' time. In the meantime, motorists were implored to assist in this process by driving along the road and even parking on it! Eventually, it was said, there would be a new carriageway to Hesketh Park aerodrome.

There were some other interesting signs of the times in May 1961. Twenty betting shops were allowed to open. The Trocadero Cinema was demolished, making way for a extension to Woolworth's. One of the dramatic societies, the Theatre Club, ceased to operate. In 1963 this was followed by the final closure of the Scala which had been used by the club in recent years.

Concern was expressed that the 1961 census showed a reduction in local population of some 2,000 people following a smaller fall ten years previously. St Anne's and Morecambe, however, boasted increases in that ten years of more than 6,000 and 4,000 respectively. On the other hand, the Whit Holiday in Southport was a great success with 12,000 cars parked on the beach and 5,700 deck chairs hired, but not quite as good as the all-time record year of 1960.

In the local elections in 1961, the Tories gained one seat but lost three, paving the way for a first Lib-Lab coalition to take over in 1962. By 1963 a new threatening external development was to excite the local political scene.

The Conservative Government had appointed Lord Beeching to review the loss-making operations of British Rail which owned almost all the country's railways. His report recommended the closure of about a third of the national rail network, particularly branch and local lines making heavy losses, including Southport's two lines to Preston and Liverpool. The Preston line's operating costs were apparently more than three times its income. It had always been in some difficulty and few voices were raised in its defence. It was finally condemned in May 1964 subject to improvement in bus services.

The Liverpool line was altogether a different matter, being much more heavily used. It was indeed making a loss of some £200,000 a year but British Rail had already improved its effectiveness by running some semi-fast trains, adjusting schedules and cutting the length of many trains from six carriages to three, thus reducing losses to a projected £100,000. Local concern, including much expressed by business in Southport, was considerable and the political parties vied with each other in their protests. It seems that the Conservatives, led by their M.P., took the lead in raising a petition with 10,000 signatures in protest. The Transport Minister, Ernest Marples, would not commit himself on the plan to close the line, repeatedly saying that he could do nothing until the railway authorities issued a notice of proposed closure. It seems that they also were not enthusiastic about the proposal, for the issue continued to be featured in local newspaper headlines through the spring and summer of 1964. Finally the Labour Party narrowly won the General Election in October and the Liverpool line was reprieved, permanently it seems. With hindsight, at any rate, this was a vital decision for Southport, which was increasingly becoming something like a shopping and seaside resort of Merseyside.

Certainly the holiday weekends continued to show good business when the weather was good. Easter in 1964 was the best for three years, with heavy road traffic and only light use of the railways. On Whit Monday it rained after hot weather previously and over the weekend car parking in the town was down from 33,000 in 1963 to 23,000.

The Labour Party was complaining that young people were leaving the town, perhaps consistently with the Essoldo Cinema being turned into a bingo and social club as cinema attendances fell. At Christmas 1963 there had been a 500% increase in holiday bookings to the continent; guest houses were suffering and flat construction was accelerating.

There was a proposal to build a 200 room luxury hotel and hall on the Lord Street site of the former terminal of the Cheshire Lines Railway, but it never matured. Nor did a scheme for a massive 30 acre leisure centre at the north end of the promenade including golf, archery, swimming and artificial skiing. There was much more local political debate about the need for a new Town Hall, but ideas of moving to the Cheshire Lines site or the Forum cinema area did not get anywhere.

There was however one very positive project at this time. A Corporation housing scheme was approved covering 27 acres at Ainsdale between Meadow Lane and Woodvale Road, including 218 semi-detached houses, 20 flats and 100 dwellings for old people. It was claimed that this would solve the housing problem in the town.

In the meantime the town's prime attraction of Lord Street continued to flourish. A civic group in 1964 promoted a significant improvement scheme involving the repainting of the canopies on the seaward side in a standardised black and white pattern which it was claimed would set off the multi-colours of the shop fronts. Some eyesores were removed and floodlighting introduced for some of the attractive buildings on the landward side. The black and white scheme has largely survived into the twenty-first century with a few exceptions of stores aiming to be different, mainly blue.

Through the 1960s in fact Southport continued to prosper reasonably well in accordance with its well established pattern, fortified no doubt by the improvements made to the marine lake area. In 1968 Pontins built their holiday camp near to Ainsdale beach, the best in the area, an event which necessarily brought new publicity to the town. Fortes announced their £250,000 scheme for redevelopment of the pier frontage to the promenade, with a new restaurant and a leisure centre including a stage and dance floor. The demolition of the old pavilion in 1970 to make way for Funland did not meet with universal approval since some people regretted the decline in live theatre but that loss would be remedied by the construction of the Southport Theatre alongside the Floral Hall a few years later by the corporation at a cost of £264,000.

Norman Wisdom came to town in the same year of 1968 to make a film and expressed his pleasure at Southport's attractions, particularly the availability of good hotel accommodation with the Palace empty and available – this in July. It was not surprising that it closed the following year for want of guests.

Sandown Court, a ten-storey block of eighty good quality flats, had been built just off the north end of Lord Street; flats were being offered for purchase on long lease from £5,000 or for rent from £450 a year. 3000 new town houses were under construction around the town and a new housing scheme at Ainsdale near the new coastal road along the track of the defunct Cheshire Line railway was approved.

Further afield, the development of a New Town at Skelmersdale promised a significant addition to Southport's immediate hinterland.

In the town centre new buildings were replacing old with external appearances which have since become notorious examples of the architectural culture of the 1960s. Even at the time there were strong expressions of dismay at the decline in standards exemplified by plain walls and sheets of glass. "No humanity and no warmth" one newspaper article complained, although the interiors were attractive enough. It was all about making money, it was said, without regard to the impact on the street. Thankfully, Lord Street escaped most of this new development with the exception of one or two stark monstrosities like Barclays Bank and Woolworth's buildings.

Despite all this physical progress, it was officially reported that there were 3,800 houses in the area without a fixed bath. Clearly, not everyone shared in progress and prosperity.

Yet the tripper trade continued to prosper. Typically good weather in July brought many thousands to the town on a non-holiday weekend, including 11,000 still by train on a Sunday as well as a massive car incursion resulting in a 4 to 5 mile queue returning on the Ormskirk road in the evening after 11,000 cars had paid to park. The sea bathing lake continued to act as a very popular substitute for the sea itself, drawing up to 8,000 people on a good Sunday. On the beach itself there were horse jumping competitions.

Of course the number of visitors to the town continued to be heavily dependent upon the weather - varying by a factor of two for the same weekend from one year to another.

So we can conclude that by the early 1970s Southport had substantially repaired the ravage wrought by the receding sea and had created in its stead a most attractive new foreshore area with a huge lake adorned by sailing boats, a great expanse of attractive gardens, and extensive amusement and leisure facilities, all to complement the greatest shopping centre in the north-west with Lord Street as its jewel in the crown. Within its broadly stable population of comparatively well-to-do people there was undoubtedly an ageing tendency. With not much industry, younger people were tending to look elsewhere.

The huge population of the town's hinterland, particularly on Merseyside, would surely continue to provide good custom for the town's fine shops as well as on-going tripper business even if overseas weather attractions were going still further to prejudice longer-stay holiday business. So it was a lively and bustling place in which to live and relax, although not exactly a seaside resort in the normal sense. But, of course, proper English resorts were going increasingly to feel the pinch caused by overseas travel and perhaps Southport was partly exempt from such depredation.

It would, however, encounter harder times in the next quarter of a century. To counter these and significantly improve the town further would require huge projects, which the old town would find it difficult to launch. It was, however, destined no longer to stand alone but to be absorbed in 1974 into Sefton Metropolitan Borough Council, a change which merits a new chapter.

A little footnote to this chapter – in March 1974 the clearance between the improved Marine Drive and the pier was being increased by inserting new sections in the pier at year a higher level, a development which had an echo in the year 2000. But before then much was to happen to the pier and elsewhere.

9

A DIFFERENT WORLD

The long century since the sea deserted Southport with devastating effect had witnessed an arduous and uneven municipal battle to fill the gaps both in the foreshore and in the town's appeal as a holiday and residential resort. The middle half of the century had seen the municipal efforts severely prejudiced by wars and depressions. Yet, throughout the whole period, the accent had been well on the positive. There had of course been some setbacks, some changes of course (as well as many fires) but these had been largely related to changing technology and tastes. However, the trend of provision of cultural and leisure amenities as well as of an attractive local environment, had in retrospect, been beneficial and enjoyable. As real incomes rose, the town's appearance, as well as its appeal to short term visitors, had improved.

In the following twenty years or so until almost the end of the twentieth century, things went pretty much into reverse. In February 1991, for instance, a long term resident of the town wrote most earnestly to the local newspaper in support of the restoration of the pier to its former glory, commenting that there was a time "when the whole sea front bustled with attractions". The dilapidated marine drive was being closed after being one-way for years, so that another piece of Victorian heritage was being lost along with the sea-bathing lake, the model village, the roller skating rink and now, most likely, the pier. The whole sea front including Pleasure Land and Happiland, was run down and second rate. Because of the privatisation of buses, the last bus-station had gone from the site of the former Cheshire Lines railway station and there was just the "ruin" of the abandoned SIBEC shopping centre in its place. He might also have noted the many run down flat buildings on the promenade, interspersed with abandoned establishments such as the Queen's Hotel. Southport was becoming known as the Last Resort.

So what had happened to bring about this sad deterioration? Well, as usual with history, it was not a simple single cause but a process with three main strands, all inter-linked. First, of course, the 1970's and 1980's witnessed the huge increase in overseas holiday travel. Yet, as we have suggested, this competition was not really as devastating for Southport as for the real seaside resorts such as Morecambe which were quite ruined. With rising real incomes and the growing regiment of cars, short-stay visitors, particularly day or even weekend trippers, could and did still come in droves. At Easter 1981 for instance over 250,000 visitors were reported and 27,000 cars on the beach over the weekend.

But in the same year Sefton Council were being criticised for only keeping the sea bathing pool open for eleven weeks in 1980 – and the wrong eleven weeks at that! The pool had fallen into neglect, so further diminishing its appeal no doubt. The Council explained that the season had been reduced because money had to be found from somewhere to meet the Government's guidelines, a subject to which we shall return. Perhaps so many of the general public had enjoyed warm water overseas or in indoor pools that they no longer cared to venture into the cool water of an open-air pool. One suggestion was that the Southport pool should be covered with a glass roof with solar panels, perhaps a hint of a Waterworld to come, but unlikely to attract investment in the depression days of the early 1980s.

At that time the sea bathing lake was in fact losing £68,000 a year and the Floral Hall theatre complex £200,000. Pleasure Land was making a profit but the Council was looking for a buyer. Even deck chairs on the beach were making a loss – there was also said to be difficulty in acquiring 500 good chairs for the 1981 season.

All these sad developments brings us to the second and third great external charges which beset Southport in this period.

Edward Heath's government of 1970-74 had left a parting present of the re-organisation of local government on the basis of increasing efficiency by reducing the number of councils. In and around the large city areas, this entailed the creation of metropolitan borough councils. In the Greater Manchester area, for instance, the northern part of Cheshire, including Altrincham, was joined to Stretford and Urmston, really suburbs of Manchester, to form Trafford, a quite artificial concoction. Similarly, Southport was joined to Formby and even Bootle, the latter clearly part of the port of Liverpool, to form Sefton.

The formation of these huge artificial council areas had various unfortunate results. First, the control of local affairs by local people was clearly diminished. Secondly, there was inevitably a tendency for the new councillors to favour the less prosperous sections of the new boroughs at the expense of the more fortunate areas. Perhaps it could be argued that this was a good thing, but it would hardly commend itself to the people of Altrincham and

Southport. In any event, it was certainly becoming impossible for the latter towns to raise money, even at their own expense, for their own local community projects; and the new borough councils were not going to help them if this meant seeming to favour them. All of this was true whatever the political complexion of the governing group of the new councils which tended to be fairly evenly balanced.

Yet this new organisation of local government can only be properly observed in the perspective of national government policy and economics. Up to 1979 there had been a broad political consensus in Britain based on the post-1945 settlement in favour of government management of economic policy positively directed to economic expansion, high employment and improved welfare, all related to a large measure of public ownership of the great utilities, railways and even some industry as well as the public provision of housing.

From 1979 onwards all this changed with the government of Mrs Thatcher. The new doctrine was monetarism which meant that the control of the money supply was the basic if not the only, tool of economic policy leaving everything else to essentially private enterprises controlled by private investors and managers who would respond appropriately to lower income taxes, with direct taxation being substantially replaced by indirect taxes such as VAT. The result of the application of this policy in the early 1980s was high interest rates and a high value of sterling resulting in the destruction of 30% of manufacturing industry with unemployment rising from 5% in 1979 to 12% by 1983 and not falling much until the late 1980s. After a short lived "Lawson" boom there was another economic crash in 1992 as the result of entering the European Monetary System at far too high an exchange rate.

The essential philosophy inspiring this policy system was the belief in the infallible efficacy and indeed wisdom of the free economic market. If private enterprise could not make a line of business or a new project pay, then they were just not worthwhile or indeed desirable. A great shadow of disbelief or even contempt therefore fell on public investment and indeed on community projects of any kind, including those organised by local authorities. So if a town like Southport was falling on hard times, it was a useless folly to support it by local public investment.

This doctrine was enforced by the strict control of public expenditure including that proposed by the new local authorities, who were clearly easier to control than the multitude of earlier councils. These new councils were not allowed to raise rates above a certain level, or they would be "capped" and their powers to invest money in capital projects except that doled out by the government were severely limited. This was what was meant by Sefton Council in 1981 in relation to "finding money somewhere" to meet the Government's Guidelines.

It is therefore hardly surprising that the principal improvements to Southport in the 1980's were comparatively minor private ventures or that the maintenance of existing public facilities was neglected. Early in the period, though, the Wayfarers Arcade was refurbished in 1981 mainly as a result of an initiative by the Merseyside County Council and Sefton MBC each contributing 12½% of the cost. The canopies on Lord Street were nearly 100 years old and were badly in need of repainting.

Sefton Council did in June 1981 spend £6,000 on temporary repairs to the 'bowl' of the sea bathing lake so as to be able to open it for a ten week season, but declared that £250,000 was needed to make it fully ship-shape. No way for such a project was in sight.

By 1985 the pier was only open for a summer season and a few days at Christmas. Even the Flower Show was making a loss of £70,000. In 1986 the town experienced its worst summer season for many years but this was blamed on the weather. A few improvements were made around the town. The Cambridge Arcade was refurbished and four fine business buildings on Lord Street were smartened up. There was also a major private initiative to fill the gap where the Forum cinema had been on Lord Street by a shopping and car parking complex.

For the first time the local newspapers were becoming somewhat dominated by stories of increasing crime and vandalism, fires and other tragedies.

Hotels were clearly having a bad time probably because those people who did come to stay had learnt to expect higher standards than the many small hotels could offer. Such establishments were being urged to merge with neighbours. The Palace and Victoria hotels had long gone, the latter replaced by a severe plain 1970s monstrosity of flats overlooking the Queen Victoria statue. We have already noted the fate of Queens Hotel. Only three big hotels survived. A statement in a planning application in

2000 declared that 900 hotel places were lost even after 1986, leaving only 1000 in the town.

Reference has been made earlier to the former Cheshire Lines railway station on Lord Street which became the Ribble Bus Company depot from 1954 to 1987. After the privatisation of bus services, the company's operations were split up between various smaller companies which did not need a central bus station. The SIBEC development company took over the site for a mixed retail centre. After the building was substantially constructed in June 1990, SIBEC went into administration and for three years the site was abandoned. Eventually, in 1993 Safeways took over and constructed a large food store. They refurbished the Lord Street frontage building and provided a number of shops which have never been occupied.

A major portion of the old Winter Gardens site now serves as a car park for Safeway. At this extremity of the Lord Street area, this in present conditions may be regarded as inevitable but the consequence is that almost all the Winter Gardens' original impressive frontage to the sea and later to the marine lake now consists of unimpressive car parks. Moreover, the Lord Street frontage is no more than an empty monument with vacant shops. Only the Cheshire Lines Railway tower remains to be impressive alongside the magnificent Garrick Theatre horrendously disfigured by Bingo Club signs at ground floor level.

In this saga of limited commercial development amidst general decline in the latter part of the twentieth century, we must not lose sight of the fact that Southport was depressed, like everywhere else and particularly the north of England, by heavy unemployment. In the town itself there was horror at the number of workless people specially young people, much greater than in the lifetime of people who could not remember the early 1930s. This was of course related to the severe decline of industry in Lancashire and of trade in Liverpool. Preston dock was closing. All this damaged the tourist business of Southport.

The need for new community projects was overwhelming but the prospect of their being launched from normal U.K. and municipal resources was remote. Help, however, was at hand from new community sources – the European Community and the U.K. Lottery. Realising this, Sefton Council eventually saw the overwhelming need and the great opportunity to launch a programme of renewal and development which would promise to repair the ravages of nature and the neglect of decades in a programme of quite extraordinary ambition.

In what follows we will not seek to quantify the respective financial contributions of the U.K. Lottery Heritage Fund, European Community funds, Sefton Council, private companies and indeed Merseyside County Council. The important fact is that very substantial public funds constituted the essential catalyst for private development.

The first significant public enterprise in the 1990s was the substantial refurbishment of the Town Hall Gardens with much attractive decorative paving and a new gardens café with open air and indoor seating. This has literally paved the way for recent quite frequent street entertainment in the summer months. At a late stage a new fountain was installed in memory of Princess Diana – one wonders whether the designers realised how much young children would enjoy running through the falling water.

Two substantial renovations were carried out on the landward side of the Marine Lake, of the Kings Gardens and of the Floral Hall and Southport Theatre complex. Pleasure Land acquired major new attractions, particularly the Traumatizer ride.

However, the really dramatic new projects have related to the seaward side of the Marine Lake where the demise of the sea bathing lake to the south of the pier and of the children's playground to the north had left large dismal and derelict areas of land. The pier itself had been closed for safety reasons since 1997 with only the short stretch over the lake available as a footpath joining up with the seaward end of the old section of Marine Drive, now called Marine Parade; the section of this road running over the lake had also been closed for safety reasons.

It was clear that before any major new development could take place on the derelict land that a major improvement needed to be made to the sea defences. The old embankment was inadequate to cope with exceptional high tides and major storms on this very flat terrain, so a great new sea wall and promenade had to be planned at a cost of £4.5 million subscribed by the European Regional Development and the U.K. government. This attractive and essential project was divided into three phases covering the entire length from Weld Road in Birkdale to Fairway near the northern Park and Ride site. The first and central phase was completed in 1999, the second, northern phase undertaken in 2000 and the third, to the south, planned for 2001, all of it destined to attract many energetic walkers.

There was general agreement also that the dismal wreck of the old pier should be reconstructed not just as a historical monument but also as a link to the new development and, above all, a renewed facility for people to take a sea promenade with refreshments at the sea end. So popular has been this project that a public appeal organised by the Southport Pier Trust in the mid 1990s has added substantially to the funds provided mainly by the European Community. With a new light railway also included, the rebuilt pier was expected to open in 2001.

Yet these important planned improvements towards the sea were really only ancillary to the massive development plans for the area between the marine lake and the sea. As a first step, Sefton Council obtained in 1992 a Derelict Land Grant to reclaim the land previously occupied mainly by the sea bathing lake and the children's playground. In 1996 Sefton Council applied to the Millennium Commission for a £20 million grant to be matched by a similar amount from public and private sector agencies. By 1997 a development contract had been let for all this area to United Reality Crowngate Ltd in a complex deal which involved the private developer building and hiring out a multiplex cinema and a leisure centre probably including a bowling alley, all on the southern side of the pier, plus Waterworld and a substantial retail capacity (mainly Matalan), together with a hotel and restaurants, on the northern site. The whole project was named Ocean Plaza. Planning permission was finally given in September 1998.

Waterworld is a kind of exciting indoor substitute for the seaside, including a beach. The concept originates from the U.S.A. and the Southport facility is due to be the first in the U.K.

Work on this extraordinarily ambitious project costing some £35m began in 1999 but was suspended in May 2000 because of a dispute between the developer and Sefton Council. This apparently arose because the developer had reappraised its financial position and concluded that the project was only viable if a greater retail element was included, a proposal which the Council found difficult. In the context of this dispute the developer, it was reported, failed to make a £8m payment due to the Council. After some delay the Council cancelled the whole contract.

At this stage foundation work had been completed on the whole site and the multiplex cinema partly built to the extent that the tiered construction of the different screen auditoria could be clearly seen, all, it was said, at a total cost of some £7m. The Council found a new developer, Greenport Estates, to continue and hopefully to complete the project, but clearly a complex financial settlement needed to be reached with the United Reality Crowngate which took until November 2000 to negotiate.

In any event, time was needed to conclude a new contract with Greenport Estates and indeed to obtain a new planning consent since the new developer also required additional retail capacity to make the project viable – i.e. profitable. It is an interesting aspect of the whole scheme that Waterworld, the principal customer attraction, is understood to be so costly to construct (at over £1 lm) and to operate that it is deemed to be necessary to hand it over capital free to the operator.

The final plan for which consent was given in October 2000 includes, on the northern area and in addition to Waterworld, three large retail units with gross internal size of 35,000, 30,000 and 20,000 square feet of which the largest is understood to be still for Matalan, and two restaurants with drive-through facilities as well, of course, as a large car parking area. On the southern site will be a huge leisure building included the multiplex cinema and a health club and possibly a bowling alley. In February 2001 a revised planning application was approved to allow an additional 10,000 square feet of retail space to be included at the mezzanine level in the form of a sports goods shop to complement the health centre on the ground floor of the leisure building. The proposed hotel is to be moved to the landward side of this site displacing the model yacht pond next to the pitch and putt course which will remain.

The new planning application forecast that Waterworld would attract 500,000 visitors in its first year of which 350,000 would be day visitors and 150,000 would stay overnight. The whole of the Ocean Plaza was expected to attract 1 million visitors a year initially. Various estimates were also given of the benefit to Southport of extra employment as well as increased spending in shops, hotels, and so on, as well as of the potential adverse initial impact on the retail trade.

We cannot here be concerned with all these detailed figures which, despite all the supposedly expert hypotheses, are essentially in the nature of looking into a crystal ball. What is beyond question is that the whole plan, including the sea-wall, the pier, Waterworld, cinema, leisure centre, shops and hotel, constitutes a seismic shift in the level of visitor attractions to the town. Certainly, some aspects will be regarded as useful and attractive to local residents, but the overriding criteria for an overall successful impact on Southport will be the number of additional visitors attracted, throughout the year, every year.

There will of course be a real opportunity for visitors to come to the new development to enjoy several of its facilities in a day and go back home. In order to benefit the town as a whole, rather than damaging its business, the new attractions when added to the existing ones – the lake, the sea, the gardens, the miniature railway, Pleasure Land and, above all, the shops especially on Lord Street, will need to attract many thousands of new visitors to stay at least one night. To believe that this will happen is great act of faith.

It will be vital for the town to treat this substantial addition to its effective area and facilities as a kind of catalyst, a spur and a challenge to improve its existing attractions so as to entice the extra visitors to come over the lake on foot or on the new pier train or on the hopefully re-opened bridge on Marine Parade which is expected to carry pedestrians, cyclists and buses. New or re-opened hotels, hotels with modern facilities and moderate charges, need to respond to, and hopefully to anticipate, the potential new demand. The many attractive cafes and restaurants charging reasonable prices will have a new opportunity to widen their appeal.

While all this somewhat dramatic renegotiation of the Ocean Plaza contract was proceeding in the summer of 2000 Sefton Council also gave planning permission for a massive retail warehouse type of development just to the east of the town centre on former railway land. ASDA is to have a food store of 70,000 square feet – getting toward the size of the largest out of town food stores – which will be accompanied by eleven retail units of around 10,000 square feet each, a modest warehouse size.

This whole development will also constitute a threat and a challenge to the existing retail business of the town. The non-food units could perhaps constitute more serious competition for the existing Meols Cop warehouse complex a mile or two further east, but ASDA could make life more difficult for existing supermarkets, although Sainsburys on Lord Street has additional attractions as a large convenience store which many people can visit on foot. Although, on the face of things, it is surprising that this further retail development should be allowed simultaneously with Ocean Plaza, it probably does not significantly prejudice it or alter the overall challenge and opportunity which the latter presents to the town. Certainly it does not offer a significant extra attraction to visitors.

What is beyond dispute is that all these new projects, undertaken or planned in the last years of the twentieth century, will ensure that the early years of the twentieth-first century will be very exciting for Southport. After a quarter of a century of stagnation and decline, the backlog of repair and neglect is being made up in one great splurge of enterprise involving at last the positive utilisation of the remaining extra land abandoned by the departing sea.

Both public and private enterprise are heavily involved. The public enterprise essentially depends on ordinary people either as taxpayers to governments who provide European funds or as voluntary but compulsive subscribers, most of them working-class people, to the UK Lottery. One has to hope and believe that in ten years' time the conclusion will be that it has all been worth while.

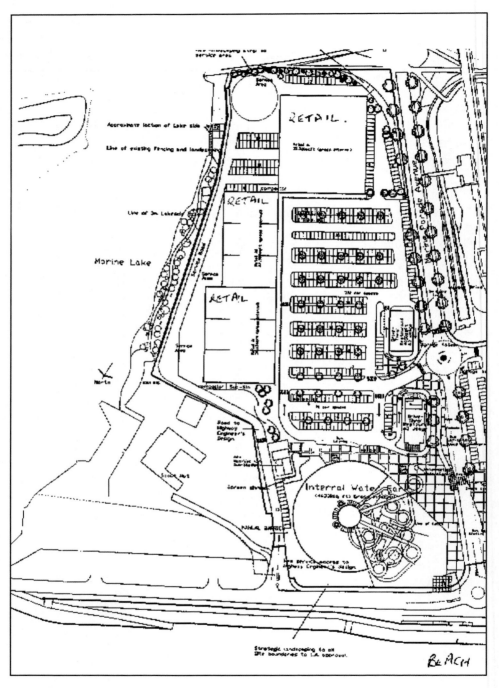

Plan of Ocean Plaza. Drawing for planning application approved Autumn 2000.

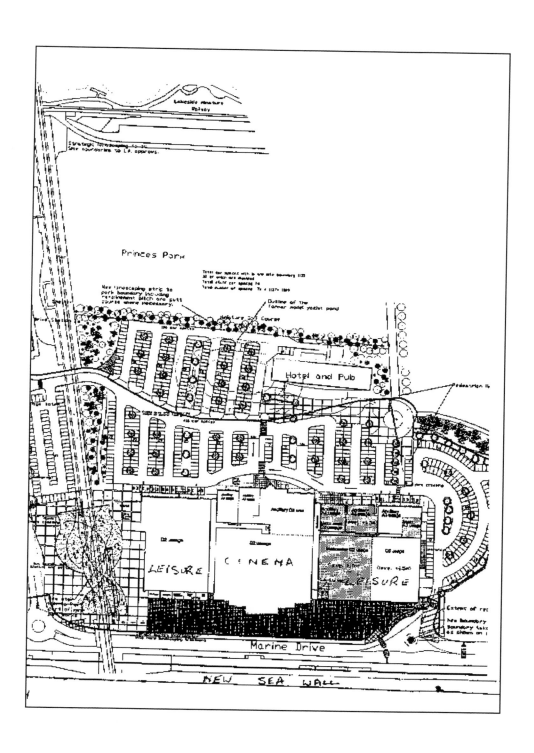

CONCLUSIONS

I feel sure, dear reader, that if you have indeed followed the real story of Southport right through, you will by now have endorsed my initial view that there was far more to it than the simplistic local histories would have us believe.

In the first place, I trust that you will now appreciate the fantastic and indeed unique flowering of the fledgling new town in less than a lifetime in the middle period of the nineteenth century and especially in the third quarter, its amazing railway age. You will now understand that there was nowhere else at all like it in the north of England, fashioned as it was by the mushrooming wealth of Lancashire in the great new industrial age.

This wealth was harnessed by the ambition and sophistication of its upper middle class residents to produce a great panoply of partly public but mainly privately financed edifices housing every kind of privileged cultural and entertainment facilities, with the whole reaching a wonderful apotheosis in the 1870s. In retrospect it seems almost a miracle that the domain of the sand dunes was so swiftly transformed into a display of unrivalled splendour adorning an unique shopping street.

Yet in that very same decade the sea, which had triggered it all, retreated from it in a display of what a more superstitious age might have regarded as a manifestation of the disdain of the gods. This astonishing departure threw the social scene into stark relief. But all was not "black and white". Already it had become surprisingly apparent that many of the thousands of "trippers" who came to the seaside were attracted also to the more sophisticated delights of places like the Winter Gardens and the museums which had clearly been provided essentially for the well-to-do local inhabitants. Yet there were soon complaints to be heard from such citizens that the entertainments were being "dumbed down".

There indeed was the rub. These great temples for leisure and learning appeared to have gone over the top in their display of the pride and ambitious self-satisfaction of the middle and upper classes. As the numbers of working class visitors fell away, largely because of the recession of the sea, these enterprises fell on harder times. Even the middle classes visited less; the Palace Hotel soon felt the pinch and later even the Winter Gardens.

From that point onwards the real story of Southport is the decade by decade account of the town's effort both to repair the damage occasioned by the retreating sea and to take advantage of the extra land it made available. In this major battle over the ravage and the offerings of nature, private enterprise was of little account since the returns on the huge investment required were too uncertain, too broad and too far ahead. Municipal enterprise became vital and yet more difficult over long periods of economic depression and war – and indeed of perverse economic policies – as well as of the emergence of overseas travel as a vast competitor. So progress was spasmodic and protracted until late in the twentieth century as new national and international support came along.

Thus we have inherited a fascinating history of a unique town battling against unique difficulties. Throughout this story it is clear that the town was by no means concerned only with the direct interests of its residents in undisturbed enjoyment of their town. Even in the mid-Victorian period those of them who wanted to disregard the interests of the visitors and the extra wealth they brought had clearly been in a minority. The strenuous efforts by local community leaders to offset the damage done by the retreating sea – particularly in the saga of the Cheshire Lines Extension Railway – represented just the early evidence of the concern of many people for the real business interests of the town. As we come to the end of our story, the hugely ambitious Ocean Plaza development can only be successful in itself and in restoring greater prosperity to the town if a minimum predicated total of a million extra visitors is achieved and surpassed.

This is not to say that Southport is unattractive at the beginning of the new millennium. Lord Street is almost always pleasant and bustling. A glimpse of the sun brings many thousands of relaxed residents and visitors to stroll through the attractive gardens and parks and around the marine lake and new sea road – as well as to park their hundreds of cars on the beach. Its special events, including the flower show, the air shows, the musical fireworks competition, its annual twenty-four hour sailing race and even the switching-on of the new Christmas lights, attract tens of thousands of people. It is truly a place of many parts. Yet it will do better with new pier and a new sea-wall to complement the great specific attractions of Ocean Plaza hopefully leading to the restoration of the dilapidated buildings on the promenade as well as the refurbishment of Hesketh Park.

An interesting indulgence open to a historian – even a local historian and particularly of Southport – is to ask the "What if?" question. What if the sea had not receded? Obviously, there would have been no marine lake with its clear advantages for safe sailing and boating. On the other hand, it can hardly be doubted that Southport could have had many more visitors who were more than day trippers – at least until overseas travel slowed things down. The attractive hotels such as the Victoria, the Palace and Queen's would surely have survived much longer at least.

More than that, however, there would surely have been created much more accommodation for people with modest means seeking seaside family holidays with reasonable entertainment facilities, not by any means as blatant as Blackpool's. Room would have been found for such accommodation outside the main town centre, perhaps amongst the sandhills. After all, Pontins came to Ainsdale, where a good beach remains, and has survived.

Now of course it is all too late. Even the massive Ocean Plaza project cannot restore a good close sandy beach although new transport facilities might connect it to Ainsdale. Yet an artificial seaside will be created in Waterworld. All in all, the resort might just get something of the best of both worlds – the marine lake and an improved seaside area, attracting visitors of varying tastes.

One thing for sure, the town which has spent well over a century with its back to the sea, is going back to face the sea.

BIBLIOGRAPHY

As explained in the Introduction, the great majority of the information in this book, or used in its production, was from the files of the local newspaper, *The Visiter*, held in Southport Library. All the staff in the Reference Library have been most helpful, particularly in the Local History Unit.

Also held in the Library are:
Southport Pier, a folder containing a compilation of sources of information, lists of newspaper references and list of the main historical events.

Southport Stage and Screen, a book written by Harold Ackroyd and produced, printed and published in 1991 by Amber Valley Print Centre.

The Southport and Cheshire Lines Extension Railway written by R.S. Toby in 1977 and published by Klofron of Norwich, which is very graphic in its assessment of the financial folly of the project and of the huge losses suffereed by its principal local backers.

Sandy Shores in South Lancashire by R. Kay Greswell, published in 1953 by London University Press, which has been the principal source of explanation of the causes and the timing of the recession of the sea.

History of Southport by F.A. Barley, published by Angus Downie in 1955, a useful general source on the nineteenth century in particular.

I have also consulted:
Old Birkdale and Ainsdale by Sylvia Harrop, published in 1985 by Birkdale and Ainsdale Historical Research Society, which is most useful on the origins of Birkdale Park.

Southport, A Pictorial History by Harry Foster, published by Phillimore in 1995, which contains a multitude of old pictures and a broad historical commentary and which has been useful in drawing attention to some key events and places.

Leeds and Liverpool Canal by Mike Clarke, published by Carnegie in 1990.

For a broader view of Victorian England, two delightful books are:
Railways and the Victorian Imagination by Michael Freeman, Yale University Press, 1999.

The Great Exhibition of 1851 by Jeffrey A. Auerback, also Yale University Press, 1999.

INDEX